"Fr Lanzetta's compact treatise p
the papal office together with an
aims, and problems of Pope Franc
cal corruption, and misleading d...
ments from the pope, he offers us reasons for continuing fidelity
to perennial Catholic doctrine as well as respectful criticism of
deviations from it. *Super Hanc Petram* is a timely gift for a storm-
tossed Church."

—Most Rev. Athanasius Schneider,
Auxiliary Bishop of Astana in Kazakhstan,
author of *Christus Vincit: Christ's Triumph
over the Darkness of the Age*

"Father Lanzetta combines theological scholarship of the first
order with extensive pastoral experience... His position is far
from both synodalism and hyperpapalism and appears as a balanced reaffirmation of the Petrine primacy amid the contemporary
chaos. This book is convincing and clear; it satisfies our need for
understanding."

—from the Foreword by Roberto de Mattei,
author of *Love for the Papacy and Filial Resistance
to the Pope in the History of the Church*

"This is a serious and important critical work on the theological
and philosophical roots of Pope Francis's thought. The author is
erudite and engaging, at times polemical. Even if not all will agree
with his interpretation of the Second Vatican Council and its
legacy, the Catholic reader—not only scholars but also theologically
interested laity—will profit by wrestling with this learned study."

—Eduardo J. Echeverria,
Professor of Philosophy and Systematic Theology
at Sacred Heart Major Seminary, Detroit,
and author of *Pope Francis: The Legacy of Vatican II*

"There can be no Church without the Pope, and no Pope without the Church. On that all Catholics agree. But complications arise when a Pope misinterprets his role, and chooses to judge—rather than to defend—the faith that the Church has always cherished. Then the relationship between Pope and Church, a relationship properly based on mutual service and submission, is broken. Father Lanzetta explores the theological implications of the conflict that we now face, as well as its possible origins."

—Philip F. Lawler,
author of *Lost Shepherd: How Pope Francis Is Misleading His Flock*

"Father Serafino Lanzetta is the type of priest that a good Catholic who really wants to sanctify himself would dream of having as a confessor or, better yet, as a spiritual director. He has solid principles, his feet on the ground, and a humble way of speaking that conquers hearts. Additionally, in his lectures and writings, he knows how to interweave systematic theology and deep spirituality. These qualities shine through in *Super Hanc Petram*, making it a rewarding read. He masterfully tackles the thorniest questions of the current crisis in the Church and in the papacy, while maintaining a supernatural perspective."

—José Antonio Ureta,
author of *Pope Francis's "Paradigm Shift": Continuity or Rupture in the Mission of the Church?*

Super Hanc Petram

Super Hanc Petram

The Pope and the Church at a Dramatic Moment in History

Serafino M. Lanzetta

Foreword by
Roberto de Mattei

Os Justi
Press

Lincoln, Nebraska

Os Justi Press
P.O. Box 21814
Lincoln, NE 68542
www.osjustipress.com

Send inquiries to
info@osjustipress.com

ISBN 978-1-960711-52-6 (paperback)
ISBN 978-1-960711-53-3 (hardcover)
ISBN 978-1-960711-54-0 (ebook)

Typesetting by Nora Malone
Cover design by Julian Kwasniewski
On the cover: Medallion of an Apostle
by Giotto di Bondone (Assisi, 1290s);
Mosaic of Pope Francis (St Paul Outside
the Walls, 2013)

Contents

Foreword

Roberto de Mattei

Father Serafino M. Lanzetta, incardinated in a diocese in the United Kingdom, combines theological scholarship of the first order with extensive pastoral experience. From this comes the balance with which, in this book, he tackles complex problems of an ecclesiological and moral order.

One of the disastrous effects of the postconciliar period has been the splitting of the theological world into two camps: on the one hand, the *nouvelle théologie*, modern and postmodern, which questions everything that predates the Second Vatican Council; on the other hand, those who adhere to the Church's Tradition but, in reaction, disregard theological currents from the 1960s on.

Father Serafino M. Lanzetta does not discount the contributions that some contemporary theologians have offered to the development of theology but gathers together and retransmits the echo of the Roman school that included Mons. Brunero Gherardini (1925–2017). The latter's groundbreaking work *The Ecumenical Vatican Council II: A Much-Needed Discussion* (published in 2009 by the Franciscans of the Immaculate) opened the way for a theological reassessment of the Church's twenty-first council. Many theses of Gherardini, considered provocative at the time, are now generally admitted to be true, and allow Father Lanzetta to confront serenely the fundamental problem of today's theological and moral crisis.

The first and most important contribution this book offers is of an ecclesiological nature. Father Lanzetta seeks to define accurately the pope's role and the institution of the papacy. He shows the danger of giving precedence to pastoral care over doctrine, to action over being, to the person of the pope over the institution of the Church. Original and interesting reflections are dedicated to the correct relationship between the pope and the Church. There is no Church without the pope, Father Lanzetta affirms, but neither is there the pope without the Church. The formula *ubi Petrus, ibi Ecclesia* must necessarily and ontologically correspond to *ubi Ecclesia, ibi Petrus*. Peter is the rock of the Church; he is the one who in himself serves as the foundation for the building up of the Church; Peter's faith is the presupposition of his constitution as a rock. "Faith is united to the person and therefore we could speak of Peter, the pope, as a believing person. Faith is the reason for his being a rock and the rock, which is his own person, is in turn based on faith in Christ and on the faith of the Church." To put Peter's personal faith before the faith of the Church is to slip into subjectivism and dogmatic relativism. Hence, there is a profound unity between the person of Peter and the faith of Peter.

Father Lanzetta's reflections on this matter are not unique but are supported many saints and theologians. In his commentary on Matthew 16:18, Saint Bruno (1045–1123, bishop of Segni, who rebuked Paschal II with the same respectful firmness with which Paul addressed Peter),[1] explains that the foundation of the Church is not Peter, but the Christian faith confessed by Peter. In fact, Christ affirms that He will build His Church not on the person of Peter, but on the faith that Peter manifested in saying: "You are the Christ, the Son of the living God." To this profession

---

[1]   See Galatians 2:11–14.

of faith Jesus responds: "It is on this rock and on this faith that I will build my Church."[2]

Naturally, we must not separate the Church from the pope to whom Jesus Christ entrusted its leadership. The primacy of the pope's governance, together with the infallibility of his magisterium, constitutes a permanent and essential element of the divine constitution of the Church to which Jesus gave a monarchical form precisely to ensure its indefectibility. It is he, and no one else, who is the supreme judge of final appeal, and never before, as at the present moment, have Catholics been in greater need of clearly defined and firm words from the Supreme Pastor to combat the attacks, internal and external, that the Church is currently undergoing. Father Lanzetta's position is far from both synodalism and hyperpapalism and appears as a balanced reaffirmation of the Petrine primacy amid the contemporary chaos.

The pages that the author dedicates to the new form of nominalism, according to which words no longer correspond to reality but are used to say something other than their original and authentic meaning, are very insightful. Nominalism was historically the highway leading to pragmatism, that is, to the dissolution of thought via the dissolution of language. The very concepts of orthodoxy and heresy evaporate in the nominalistic primacy of praxis. In this respect, more than the spread of heresy, the real problem of the Church today consists in what Father Lanzetta accurately defines as a "liquid apostasy." It has its roots in the attempt to separate "the doctrinal aspect of Revelation from the pastoral one, seeing the beginning of preaching not in the truths to be believed but in how to believe, judging its appropriateness and modalities."

---

[2]   *Commentary on Matthew*, pars III, chap. XVI, in *PL* 165:213.

Super Hanc Petram

Father Lanzetta's book is convincing and clear; it satisfies our need for understanding. Theology is a sacred science that should be dear to all Catholics, priests and lay people, wanting to deepen their understanding of the truths of the Catholic faith and morality. Those wishing to gain doctrinal and spiritual benefit from the truths of the Gospel must listen humbly to the words of those who have dedicated their lives to explaining Church teaching, never deviating from sound doctrine.

Preface

In the year 2013 a singular image was engraved forever in the memory of Catholics: an exhausted pope, leaving the Vatican by helicopter. He had resigned. He expected his successor to be elected, and so he was. He came "from the other side of the world" and took the name of Francis, after St. Francis of Assisi. At this time there was, in particular, a great hope that a more energetic and younger successor of Peter, with a determined approach, could steer the Church, afflicted by many scandals, back on course. The newly elected pope was greeted with great warmth, along with an increasing—almost feverish—expectation, fueled by the media, of a turning point that he would initiate, not only in the structure of the Roman Curia, but also in the doctrinal sphere. It was time to change radically and "remove the remnants of the past."[3] And thus, since the election of Jorge Mario Bergoglio as bishop of Rome and Supreme Pontiff, "nothing has been the same as before."[4] However, while the pope's popularity has grown exponentially, the popularity of the Church and the Christian message has not grown quite as much. The vitality indexes of the Church are very

---

[3] Giuseppe Dalla Torre, *Papi di famiglia. Un secolo di servizio alla Santa Sede* (Venice: Marcianum Press, 2020), 137.

[4] Dalla Torre, *Papi di famiglia*, 137.

low and continue to dwindle. This does not bode well for the future. What happened?

It seems that there has been a sort of identification of the pope *with* the Church, together with a real distancing of Francis *from* the Church as it has been up until now. This is apparent in his urgent request that the Church "go out" (of herself) to become a "people on the move," so as to be permanently configured as a "synodal Church," an echo and a realization of a "conciliar Church." This novelty does not necessarily take as a model the missionary Church seeking to make all men disciples of Christ, nor does it spare much thought for the teachings on faith and morals as transmitted by the constant magisterium. Acting in a more up-to-date way, adapted to the present time, is presented as justifying the pastoral shift. However, this is also and above all a doctrinal turning-point. In this book we will analyze the various areas of Francis's magisterial discourse. As will be seen, it always tends toward accommodation, is respectful of a plurality of positions—even when these should be denounced and corrected for their lack of orthodoxy—and as a rule encourages change. A "static, immobile, rigid" Church does not suit Francis's fancy. Conversely, on one thing and one thing only is the Argentine Pontiff inflexible: the postconciliar liturgical reform. Of Vatican II itself, Francis does not always profess to be a faithful executor, referring *expressis verbis* to the conciliar documents. Instead, he prefers to focus on its "spirit." Yet in the domain of liturgy, his meaning is unmistakable and intransigent: "After this magisterium, after this long journey, we can affirm with certainty and with magisterial authority that the liturgical reform is irreversible."[5] With *Traditionis*

---

[5]   Pope Francis, Address to Participants in the 68th National Liturgical Week, August 24, 2017, in *L'Osservatore Romano*,

Custodes, this lead to an unprecedented condemnation not only of the Mass according to the Missal of 1962, but of the *lex orandi* itself that preceded the new Missal of Paul VI. Ultimately, a *lex orandi* founded on a *lex credendi* with very blurred contours leaves room for uncertainty, and can only benefit a "*lex dubitandi.*"

What has become of the Church in herself, as willed by her divine Founder? What is the role of the pope in the Church? These are fundamental questions, but they now seem to be irrelevant. The question of two popes in the Church, one emeritus and one reigning, based on an unfortunate distinction, then driven by some commentators into an additional but surreptitious division between *munus* and *ministerium*, has further complicated the topic. It has generated doubt about the unicity of Peter as the foundational rock. Not only has it become difficult to know who the pope is, considered in the *munus* proper to him, when, instead of the rock on which the Church is built, Peter seems to have become a stumbling block, but furthermore, it has become difficult to identify even who the "true" pope is. The scenario that presents itself is very disturbing, and our faith in Peter and in the Church is deeply wounded as a result. Those most adversely affected are the faithful. They are tossed about by the diverging winds of pastoral cliques (linked mostly to partisan interests), and wonder if and how Jesus's words can still be applicable to the Church today: "You are Peter, and on this rock I will build

---

August 25, 2017, p. 8. Throughout this work, magisterial texts will be quoted and translated from their original printed source. An English online version is available at www.vatican.va. Between our translation and the online version there could be slight differences, but never to the point of changing the meaning of the text. With a more literal translation, several nuances are kept so that the whole meaning can be grasped more accurately.

my Church, and the gates of Hades shall not prevail against it" (Mt 16:18). Where is the rock?

We must, therefore, understand in what way Peter is *kepha*—in name and in fact, by virtue of his faith in Christ—to be able to grasp if and under what conditions this rock might be allowed to crumble without the Church itself crumbling. We must reflect on this pair of realities, pope-Church, and show their profound unity in a hierarchical relationship. This relationship includes distinction, with not Peter, but Christ, at its center; Peter is dependent upon Christ and the Church. The love and honor due to the pope is indisputable, amplified to the utmost with the dogma of the Roman Pontiff's infallibility. All this is certainly Catholic and must remain so. But one cannot deny the risk of excess—of accentuating the role of the pontiff to such an extent that the Church, and thus the Faith, is seen as in some way dependent on him as an individual man. In reality, it is the pope who depends on the Church and on her faith, and not the opposite. His action should be circumscribed within the confines of the mystery-Church of which he is the foundation, within the confines of the Church's doctrine of faith and morals. The Church in some way precedes the pope in her being constituted as *ekklesia* and as a salvific body on the foundation of the Twelve by virtue of the offering of the Body of Christ. The pope is the servant of this mystery, for he must preserve its unity and never propose a confused multiplicity of teachings, even if speciously justified in the name of pastoral action.

Combined with a mistaken fusion of the pope's person and the mystery-Church, in Francis's pontificate there has been an attempt at a general revision of the previous magisterium and of crucial matters in faith and morals. It is difficult to say what Francis has not meddled with. There is nothing wrong with a pope refining an existing doctrine, but the new must be in continuity with what precedes it, and any development must be homogeneous. Otherwise, it is more than just a development; it is actually a corruption of doctrine. This book reflects critically on various interventions from Francis which require clarification urgently. Timely correction is needed on the part of those whose duty this is, because, in my opinion, they constitute a clear break with previous teaching.

We will explore Francis's concept of mercy. It is based on the one hand on the supposed inevitability of sin, which the Son made His own as He "contaminates" Himself by making Himself to be sin,[6] and on the other hand, on the impossibility of *not* being forgiven, since the gates of heaven are opened to everyone, even to Judas. The Abu Dhabi Statement serves as a guideline for *Fratelli Tutti*: God *wills* all religions as He *wills* the diversity of sex, race, and language. If one religion is as good as another, then Christ is only a social Good Samaritan serving humanity. It is thus that we consider *Fratelli Tutti*, in which Christ is absent and cedes His place to this humanity. Also, we reflect on the abolition of the teaching on the death penalty, which seems to be an unprecedented severing of a branch reaching all the way back to the apostles Peter and Paul. While everything else seems to be falling apart, there remains, as mentioned, only one cast-iron certainty: the liturgical reform that followed Vatican II. This liturgical outlook, nevertheless, must be framed in the broader context of Francis's understanding of Vatican II, so that it can be seen in its proper context.

Next, there are also other areas with which the Pontiff has meddled, which it is appropriate to highlight and which we sketch for further consideration. For example, there is the 2015

---

[6]   See, among other examples, Pope Francis, Angelus of February 14, 2021, in *L'Osservatore Romano*, February 15, 2021, p. 8.

intervention on matrimonial nullities with its double motu proprio (one for the Latin Church and one for the Eastern Church), for the sake of speeding up the canonical process. Is this an improvement of the Code of Canon Law or has it only destabilized marital indissolubility, as well as producing new and unresolved juridical problems? It creates a real hodgepodge in the bigger picture.[7] It has rightly been said that "canonical science, in the face of this reformist season, extremely extensive and varied as well as not without uncertainties and some conflicts, has generally appeared disoriented if not disconcerted, almost prey to a paralyzing crisis of identity...."[8]

It is enough to consider the number of *motu proprio*s produced by this pontificate to gauge Francis the reformist's intentions. If we consider the large supply of ecologically focused productions, from *Laudato Si'* to the Synod on the Amazon and the various speeches on the subject, we can observe a paradigm shift in the social magisterium. The notion of integral ecology, which had man at its center, as the sole creature to be made in the image and likeness of the Creator, has now become the ecology of the Earth, of nature, while man is somehow criminalized, together with all modern technology, for having exploited "Mother Earth." If the Earth takes the place of man, what will be the theological and moral standard of the social magisterium? The Earth without man portrayed in *Laudato Si'* is man without Christ in *Fratelli Tutti*.

---

[7] See Geraldina Boni, *La recente attività normativa ecclesiale: 'finis terræ' per lo 'ius canonicum'? Per una valorizzazione del ruolo del Pontificio Consiglio per i testi legislativi e della scienza giuridica nella Chiesa* (Modena: Mucchi, 2021), 73. In note 5 on p. 66, Boni's specific studies on this subject are listed.

[8] Boni, 7.

This book also aims to identify critically, through the lens of systematic theology, the roots of Francis's theological thought. Some have adopted an "intellectual approach" to the complex figure of Pope Francis, attempting to identify his influences and debunk the myth of a Bergoglio shallow or incapable in theology. Yet this approach does not adequately distinguish between magisterium, theology, and philosophy, nor does it adequately discern what must follow from the pope's own teachings. There is an interweaving of magisterium and theology, in which personal opinions are presented as authentic teaching and vice versa. However, here to be sure, the reality is superior to the idea. And ideas must be judged through reality and never the other way around. Far from trying to substantiate the hypothesis of an Argentine, Peronist, and anti-Western pope, undernourished due to a meager theological diet, our purpose is simply to offer a serene evaluation of certain of his teachings. Their specific social and intellectual background, though undoubtedly present, is irrelevant to an overall judgment about the truth of what the pope teaches. Therefore, we are careful to offer a reading of the current magisterial data so that we can shoulder the task of unearthing the questions—sometimes buried beneath the doctrine of authority—that are racking not only theology, but also the very substance of many people's faith. For there are some who, disheartened, abandon the Church or are ready to embrace apocalyptic views, which distract them from the real issues.

Massimo Borghesi was correct when he wrote: "Bergoglio represents in his apparent simplicity a complex figure. He himself is, in his personality, a *complexio oppositorum*."[9] The dialectical

---

[9] Massimo Borghesi, *Jorge Mario Bergoglio: Una biografia intellettuale* (Milan: Jaca Book, 2017), 25. "Bergoglio's dialectic is, unlike Hegel's, an 'open' dialectic. Because its syntheses are always

model is dear to Bergoglio and is the focus he has been developing since the years of his preparation for the priesthood. Francis's antinomian thought was influenced by his study of Gaston Fessard (1897–1978), a Jesuit of the School of Lyon and a friend of Henri de Lubac, who himself was influenced not by Hegel but by the philosophy of action of Maurice Blondel.[10] Blondel made immanence his philosophical principle.[11] Fessard wrote *La dialectique des "Exercices spirituels" de saint Ignace de Loyola* (Paris, 1956), which has had a strong influence on the future pope.[12] This is where we primarily find the philosophical roots of Francis's thought and his actions.

Finally, another question is helpful to raise: what will become of theology after Francis? Not only is the Magisterium currently under attack, but also theology as a science. Rather than a magisterial teaching *strictu sensu*, Francis's theological interpretation of dogma is a personal vision of the pope's that is often very social and political in nature. It seems that the "theology of the people," an Argentine variant of liberation theology developed by Lucio

---

provisional, they must always be supported and reconstructed, and because reconciliation is the work of God, not primarily of man. This explains his criticism of a 'self-referential' Church, closed in its own 'immanence,' marked by the double temptation of Pelagianism and Gnosticism. The Christian is 'de-centered,' the point of equilibrium between opposites being outside of him" (ibid., 26).

[10] See Borghesi, *Bergoglio*, 33–36. See also Juan Carlos Scannone, "La filosofia dell'azione di Blondel e l'agire di Papa Francesco," in *La Civiltà Cattolica* (2015) IV, 216–33.

[11] See Roberto de Mattei, "Il modernismo: radici e conseguenze storiche," in *Vecchio e nuovo modernismo: Radici della crisi nella Chiesa*, ed. idem (Rome: Fiducia, 2020), 29–30.

[12] See Borghesi, *Bergoglio*, 33.

Gera, is what inspires Pope Bergoglio.[13] The people (of God, of a nation?) was first a "mystical" category; Francis changed it to a "mythical" one. In the judgment of Gian Enrico Rusconi, this is "a significant example of the semantic mobility of Pope Bergoglio, which is not always easy to follow."[14] Rusconi also emphasizes something more fundamental, realized in Bergoglio's pontificate: the birth of a narrative theology and a new theological school. By "narrative theology" he means a "new religious hermeneutic, centered on the omnipresent and all-encompassing evocation of God's mercy"; a "semantic reinvention, emotional expressiveness accompanied by conceptual flexibility, leading to a language rich in metaphors, congruent with the Gospel parables."[15] (It must be noted, however, that, though Jesus explained the parables to His disciples, Bergoglio instead prefers not to respond to those who raise doubts about his approach.)

The Bergoglian narrative of the Faith follows a toned-down, de-dramatizing type of logic based on mercy, which does not take into account the necessary reparation-expiation of sin.[16] In this metaphorical narrative, almost always bordering on the un-orthodox, always flirting with equivocation, the meaning of words change and with them the entire discourse. We are confronted with a neo-nominalism, which seeks to redefine theological concepts established by a very long tradition. This leaves listeners from time to time perplexed and discouraged (if conservative or traditionalist), or edified and iron-clad "hyperpapalists" (if more

---

[13] See Walter Kasper, *Papa Francesco: La rivoluzione della tenerezza e dell'amore* (Brescia: Queriniana, 2015), 99–100.

[14] Gian Enrico Rusconi, *La teologia narrativa di papa Francesco* (Bari: Laterza, 2017), 30.

[15] Rusconi, 4.

[16] Rusconi, 18–21.

progressive or even non-believing). The discourse is true or false, acceptable or not, on the basis of the prior qualification of the auditors, as in a stadium with fans of opposing teams.

Do we possess the correct tools to understand what is happening? That is what I hope to put forward with this study. Without any subversive or reactionary intent, but with filial respect for the highest authority, for the welfare of the Church and of souls, I am careful to lay out these very serious problems. I ask, with humility and faith in the Church, that they be taken seriously by those whose duty it is to do so. I will also be ready to correct the content of this book if it is erroneous or differs from Catholic truth. At all events, I hope answers may be found in conformity with the Church's faith. The *Christifideles* demand clarity: their eternal salvation is at stake.

Serafino M. Lanzetta
Portsmouth, UK
March 19, 2023
Solemnity of St Joseph

1

The Pope

"The Church not only has the obligation to be missionary, but mission is its very essence,"[17] wrote Hans Urs von Balthasar, commenting on Henri de Lubac's short treatise, *Theological Foundation of the Missions* (1946). According to the French Jesuit, the Church is catholic in that it recognizes itself as being universal *de jure*, while also desiring to be so *de facto*. In order that there would always be this missionary zeal to go out to all nations, baptizing them and making of them disciples of Christ (cf. Mt 28:19–20), the Lord gave His Church a central driving force and a firm foundation: the pope. Peter is the "rock" on which the Church is built (cf. Mt 16:18), the "permanent and visible source and foundation of unity of faith and communion" (*Lumen Gentium* 18)[18] and of the unity and indivisibility of the episcopate.[19] The Church is first *built* upon the foundation of Peter and the Apostles united with him, prior to being *sent forth* to all peoples, as the Son is sent by the Father (cf. Jn 20:21). The hierarchical institution precedes any missionary action and thus grounds it in its universal identity. From a clear concept of what the pope is

[17] Hans Urs von Balthasar, *The Theology of Henri de Lubac* (San Francisco: Ignatius Press, 1991), 45.
[18] In a note referring to the First Vatican Council, Dogmatic Constitution on the Church of Christ *Pastor Æternus*, in DH 3050s.
[19] DH 3057.

in relation to the Church we may also draw a distinct notion of what the mission of the Church is—without, however, the two dimensions being confounded with one another and dissolving together. We must begin from the essence of the thing in order to understand its operation.

The theme of the Church's mission has been a central point throughout the pontificate of Pope Francis. Nevertheless, simultaneously there have been doubts and uncertainties about whether or not the Church still has the will to be missionary, in accordance with what it was always believed to be. The mission that Francis wants to assign to the Church is an attempt to reconfigure the role of the papacy in the Church and the Church itself, viewed essentially as a people on the move. A key phrase is "pastoral conversion," which is to be adopted and indeed adapted in accordance with various doctrinal demands. This pastoral conversion is entwined with the conversion of the papacy as such, in an ecclesiological framework. It seems that while the figure of Pope Francis stands out on the world stage, the role of the pope and the divine institution of the papacy have been obscured. There is a noticeable rift between person and ministry.

Do the years of Pope Francis's pontificate lead to a new configuration of the ancient Catholic Church? This was the question posed in 2018 by Andrea Riccardi, a devoted and attentive observer of the Bergoglian pontificate, who referred to Francis as "the first 'global pope.'"[20] Francis is a pope who does not want a Church that remains entrenched in a centralist position based on her traditional principles, but which chooses to go to the peripheries of the world and to reach out to all people, above

[20] Andrea Riccardi, ed., *Il cristianesimo al tempo di papa Francesco* (Bari: Laterza, 2018).

all by means of a strong mass-media presence.[21] More recently, however, without referring to the pontificate of Francis, Riccardi has written that the "Church is burning." This is a vivid image reminiscent of the burning of Notre Dame Cathedral in Paris. It depicts in a blunt but true way the current crisis of Christianity, which is unprecedented, manifested in a slow but steady decline in its vitality index.[22]

Christians are all in the same boat. If the Church is on fire, the papacy should not be rejoicing. These two realities go together to the extent that you cannot have one without the other. The same shift "from the center to the peripheries" also appears to have been realized regarding the doctrine of the papacy itself, with a considerable emphasis placed on the collegiality and synodality of the Church. Doctrinal matters are disregarded without, however, renouncing disciplinary and pastoral interventions. These, on the other hand, manifest the strong entrenchment of pontifical authority. Francis's announced aim has been to "decentralize" the Church's authority, as seen in *Evangelii Gaudium*, the agenda-setting document of his pontificate. He invokes a "conversion of the papacy," as an application of a broader "pastoral conversion" of the central structures of the Church.[23] This conversion corresponds to an "outgoing" Church with a "missionary spirit." Starting from John Paul II's request that there should be found "a way of exercising the primacy which, while in no way renouncing what is

---

[21] Andrea Riccardi, "La Chiesa tra centri e periferie," in idem, *Il cristianesimo al tempo di papa Francesco.*

[22] Andrea Riccardi, *La Chiesa brucia. Crisi e futuro del cristianesimo* (Bari: Laterza, 2021).

[23] Pope Francis, Apostolic Exhortation on the Proclamation of the Gospel *Evangelii Gaudium* (November 24, 2013), no. 32; *AAS* 105 (2013): 1033–34.

essential to its mission, is nonetheless open to a new situation,"[24] Francis asks that this desire be achieved above all by a clarification of the ways in which Episcopal Conferences are subjects of specific attributes, including genuine doctrinal authority.[25]

At the theological level, the proposal for a more pastoral and sacramental papacy, less centered on the power of jurisdiction and magisterium, had already been made, for example, in the book by Severino Dianich.[26] However, it is not easy to grasp to what extent the *proprium* of the *munus petrinum*, which is "to shepherd," that is, to govern the Church and to confirm the brethren in the Faith, can be converted into a more pastoral and less doctrinal role. It leads to a "pastorality of doctrine" as Richard Gaillardetz[27] explains, quoting Christoph Theobald.[28] Here, the doctrinal and dogmatic contents of the Faith are subordinated to the *kerygma*. One could thus fall into a sort of pastoral opportunism, adapting the contents of the Faith for the sake of the *kerygma*, such that the latter is not subordinated to the precedence of the Faith, nor considered as its clear and integral proclamation. The "hierarchy of truths in Catholic doctrine" invoked by *Unitatis Redintegratio* 11

---

[24] Pope John Paul II, Encyclical Letter on Commitment to Ecumenism *Ut Unum Sint* (May 25, 1995), no. 95; *AAS* 87 (1995): 977–78.

[25] Pope Francis, *Evangelii Gaudium*, no. 32.

[26] Severino S. Dianich, *Per una teologia del Papato* (San Paolo: Cinisello Balsamo, 2010).

[27] Richard Gaillardetz, "The 'Francis Moment': A New Kairos for Catholic Ecclesiology," in *Proceedings of the Catholic Theological Society of America* 69 (2014): 75–80.

[28] Christoph Theobald, "The Theological Options of Vatican II: Seeking an 'Internal' Principle of Interpretation," in *Vatican II: A Forgotten Future, Concilium* 4 [English] (2005): 87–107, cited in Gaillardetz, "The 'Francis Moment,'" 76n38.

would support a "pastoral ministry in a missionary style [which] is not obsessed with the disjointed transmission of a multitude of doctrines to be insistently imposed."[29] Hence it would be a matter of interpreting the doctrines and presenting them according to the most convincing interpretation, not forgetting the role of mercy.[30] If there is no truth, only its interpretation will remain.

In reality, this effort to give precedence to pastoral care over doctrine, that is, to acting over being, to mission over the mystery-Church, causes a problem. This emphasis on action, due to its lack of clarity and its ill-defined contours, causes greater uncertainty and actually brings missionary activity to a standstill. Mission becomes soul-searching because it is deprived of its essence, namely, fidelity to maintaining the spiritual life. We end up condemning any efforts at making disciples (*matheteúsate*, Jesus's imperative in Mt 28:19, and the essence of all missionary endeavor), because the *kerygma* would no longer be the necessary proclamation of definitive salvation in Christ by means of the Church He founded, but rather an indefinite assemblage of ideas and suggestions offered to the world, often in a way designed to appear more presentable or acceptable to the world. In the absence of a definite line between the papacy and the Church, it is easy for the two to overlap and dissolve into one another; the papacy may then override the gospel.

The greatest risk that the papacy runs during Pope Francis's pontificate is precisely that of a superimposition of the person of the pope on the whole Church, an ecclesiological personalism,[31]

---

[29] Pope Francis, *Evangelii Gaudium*, no. 35; *AAS* 105 (2013): 1034.
[30] See Gaillardetz, "The 'Francis Moment,'" 78.
[31] "It is a serious mistake to imagine the papacy as an *authoritarian* office from which the pope issues imperious decisions that reflect his will alone. Rather, the Petrine Office is an *authoritative* office

albeit with the intention of displaying humility and poverty. It aims to revamp the image of the pope, to highlight better the Church's mission. Moreover, from the very name that Francis adopted—a name that "says it all"—a debate has been sparked about what is charismatic or regards personal opinion (and therefore does not properly pertain to the pope as such), and what, instead, is a distinguishing characteristic of the papal office, and so does not pertain to the temporary inspiration of the Holy Spirit. In Francis there has arisen a fundamental conflict between institution and charism. The charism, which is the "Franciscan" aspect of his pontificate, has emerged and imposed itself on his Petrine ministry. The charismatic mission of St. Francis and his love for poverty have in some way replaced, in Pope Francis, the *munus* of the one who should show no partiality for any particular charism but rather discern and establish all of them—all the while remaining above them, ensuring that the Church never lacks either the one true faith or the right direction to follow. When inspiration replaces the *munus*, rather than producing a pastoral conversion of the papacy, this leads to a change in the language of the magisterium, an expression of the papacy's more pastoral tendency; thus, the pathway of a loquacious spontaneity is entered into, in which Simon emerges more clearly than Peter. And precisely because this communication is spontaneous and subjective, it requires external support, which is very often found in the channels of communication.

To complicate the matter, there is the issue of Pope Benedict XVI's resignation (may he rest in peace). This unfortunately

---

whose holder is the custodian of an *authoritative* tradition. He is the servant of that tradition, that body of doctrine and practice, not its master." George Weigel, *The Next Pope. The Office of Peter and a Church in Mission* (San Francisco: Ignatius Press, 2020), 42.

contributed much to rendering the ecclesial situation even more confused, giving rise to suspicions about its validity, even allowing for full-blown conspiracy theories about whether he had actually retired or not. According to proponents of "Benevacantism," the formula of the resignation, written in pedantic Latin, would *de facto* contain Benedict's supposed non-renunciation, so that he could remain a watchful sentinel, albeit remotely, and, in any case, would show himself to be the true pope at a moment of decadence in the Church caused by his successor. Such a thesis also benefits from the marked discontinuity between Benedict XVI and Francis. If Francis had taught the Faith with clarity and unambiguously, the idea of the invalidity of Pope Ratzinger's resignation would not, perhaps, even have surfaced.

Yet how would Benedict XVI manifest that he is the true pope, since his decision was to remain on the sidelines and not intervene in decisive moments of the Church's life, as in the *impasse* caused by *Amoris Lætitia* and his silence about the *dubia* of the four Cardinals? Benedict would retain only a *munus spirituale* while that of governing the Church would pass on to his successor. In this theory, not only is the *munus petrinum*, which is indivisible, thus split in two, but at the same time the theological idea of a "true pope" is based on a spiritual pontificate, not visible, which is contrary to the dogma of the visibility of the Church and the ministry of the successor of St. Peter. Now that Benedict is deceased, these questions no longer pose the same kind of threat, but they are still worth discussing for theological reasons.

At the canonical level, a distinction between *munus* and *ministerium* has been postulated.[32] Benedict would have renounced the

---

[32] See Stefano Violi, "La rinuncia di Benedetto XVI tra storia, diritto e coscienza," in *Rivista Teologica di Lugano* 18, no. 2 (2013): 203–14.

ministry but not the *munus*, because of the *declaratio* with which the Pope Emeritus (the new title that Benedict XVI assigned to himself, not without causing further problems for the canonical structure of the papacy[33]) renounced his Petrine office. Moreover, Ratzinger, departing from the provisions of can. 332 §2, would have only partially renounced the *executio muneris* (which would be executed not only by words and deeds, but also by suffering and praying) and not the *munus* as such. In fact, Pope Benedict declared that he was renouncing the "ministry of the bishop of Rome, Successor of St. Peter."[34] There is no place for divisibility between *munus* and ministry, and indeed, the *declaratio* in its entirety presents these as one single thing, in accordance with what has always been understood throughout the history of the papacy. The dual *munus* thesis gained some popularity because of the last General Audience of Benedict XVI. In that final public address, Pope Benedict explained in theological terms what motivated his choice to step down but not to abandon the Church. He said he renounced "the active exercise of the ministry," which did not revoke the "always" of his *munus*, because it was "for ever."[35] However, this distinction does not work at the canonical or sacramental level and therefore inevitably leads us to understand the *declaratio* as the renunciation of the *munus petrinum* as such. This *munus* is,

---

[33] See Gianfranco Ghirlanda, "Cessazione dall'ufficio di Romano Pontefice," in *La Civiltà Cattolica*, March 2, 2013, pp. 445–62.

[34] Benedict XVI, *Declaratio Summi Pontificis—De muneris Episcopi Romæ, Successoris Sancti Petri abdicatione*, in *AAS* 105 (2013): 239. The entire *declaratio* confirms Benedict's desire to avoid separating the *munus* from the ministry, as is apparent from the title.

[35] Benedict XVI, General Audience (February 27, 2013) in *Insegnamenti di Benedetto XVI*, vol. 9 (Vatican City: Libreria Editrice Vaticana, 2013), 271–72.

in point of fact, neither an "always" nor a "for ever," in contrast to the sacrament of Holy Orders which confers a permanent character. Instead, it is a ministry that is lost either through death or through resignation.[36] This may explain why there has been some speculation regarding the validity of the resignation, despite the fact that Benedict XVI repeatedly confirmed the voluntary nature of his resignation.

All these speculations contributed to deepening doubts about the papacy as such. There has also been talk of a "shared papacy," almost as a sort of "Petrine collegiality," which was keenly desired by the advocates of the collegial shift in the Church after Vatican II.[37] As a matter of fact, until very recently, we were in a *sui generis* situation with a Pope Emeritus, claimed by some still to be the pope at all costs and against his will, and a reigning pope, who did nothing but cause confusion since assuming the sacred office. The papacy and the Church bear the brunt of all this drama. Beyond the personal ideas or political choices of the pope, what truly matters is *who the pope is* and *what the Church is*: these alone endure.

Such a consideration may also provide a response to the apocalyptic scenario that would emerge if a pope tried to paddle upstream, working against the Church, becoming a stumbling

---

[36] For a synthesis of the recent debates on this topic, see Roberto de Mattei, *Love for the Papacy and Filial Resistance to the Pope in the History of the Church* (Brooklyn, NY: Angelico Press, 2019), 142–45.

[37] To delve more deeply into the various historical-theological attempts aimed at altering the doctrine of the papacy according to the guidelines of the innovators, see Roberto de Mattei, *Vicario di Cristo: Il primato tra normalità ed eccezione*, 2nd ed. (Verona: Fede & Cultura, 2018).

block, rather than the foundation stone he is meant to be. I will therefore examine the Petrine ministry, dividing my reflection into four parts: I will first analyze the meaning of Jesus's words to Peter after the confession of Caesarea Philippi, a clear reference to the building of the Church upon Peter; then I will consider Peter in his being as *Kepha*, the rock of the Church; then the unity, in Peter, of the person and of the Faith as the foundation *stone*; finally, the relationship between the *munus petrinum* and the pope's infallible magisterium. All this will lead us to see clearly the relationship between the pope and the Church. The "*ubi Petrus ibi Ecclesia*" must necessarily *and* ontologically correspond to the "*ubi Ecclesia ibi Petrus.*"

"You are Peter"

The first teaching that we must study, which firmly establishes Petrine authority in the Church, is revealed in Jesus's words to Peter: "You are Peter, and on this rock I will build my Church, and the gates of Hades shall not prevail against it" (Mt 16:18). In the Greek we can see the distinction between "Peter" and "rock" (*sù eî Pétros e epì taúte tê pétra*), with a proper noun designating the person and a common noun designating the thing, even though the two words don't necessarily correspond to each other. Instead, the correspondence emerges from Jesus's second assertion, in His words: "on this rock." It is a phrase originally formulated in Aramaic, in which the proper noun does not differ from the noun *Kepha*. Jesus twice said: "You are *Kepha*, and on this *Kepha* I will build my Church."[38] Essentially, this means that Peter is the "Rock" by identity and by calling.

---

[38] See Oscar Cullmann, *Peter, Disciple-Apostle-Martyr: A Historical and Theological Study* (London: SCM Press, 1953), 185. According

The Pope

Oscar Cullmann rejects a widespread hypothesis that Matthew 16:17–19 is not genuine but was absent in the original and
inserted only later under the influence of demands emanating
from Rome. He also rejects the thesis according to which the
verses are spurious, meaning that Matthew would have repeated
words coming not from Jesus, but invented by the Church. The
various hypotheses formulated by Karl Goetz, Rudolf Bultmann,
and Maurice Goguel with this view are unlikely to be true due to
the scarcity of historical data on which they are based. Conversely,
the fact that in the New Testament itself there are already traces
of Jesus's words addressed to Peter is highly significant (cf. Gal
1:16–18 and 2:9).[39] Cullmann maintains that the context in which
Jesus's words are addressed to Peter is not that of the Gospel of
Matthew, but of Luke 22:31–34, in which Jesus prays for Peter,
who is being subjected to temptation. Jesus tells him that, once he
has converted, he should confirm his brethren. The context is the
Passion and the Last Supper; thus it does not call into question the
Palestinian origin of these words, but sheds a clearer light on the
meaning of Christ's will to build His *ekklesia* (a stumbling block
of Protestant exegesis in recognizing its authenticity).[40] However,
in Cullmann's judgment, Jesus's words to Peter have only a limited
historical value as they are addressed only to the person of the
apostle, and exclude any reference to his successors. On the basis
of a pure exegesis of the text, one could not see any reference to
the papacy,[41] although the Church—Cullmann maintains—is

to Cullmann (186), the Semitic character of this expression is
confirmed by other remarks, including the designation of Peter
as "*bar-yônâ*" (Mt 16:17).

[39] Cullmann, *Peter*, 184–86.
[40] Cullmann, 183; 190.
[41] Cullmann, 207–12.

11

destined to continue over time, even if it is not identified with the Kingdom of God, but is simply striving towards it.[42]

However, it is difficult to understand how one could reconcile the permanency of the Church, against which the gates of hell will not prevail, with an impermanence of the Petrine succession. The event of the Church's foundation, according to the judgment of the Reformed theologian, would be a fundamental event like the incarnation of the Word; it occurred once and for all.[43] Yet Cullmann himself acknowledges that a complete study of the patristic interpretation of the words of Jesus in question would be useful.[44] In fact, this is the key to overcoming an apparent historical deadlock, something inevitable with the Lutheran conception of the Scriptures. It is in fact inaccurate to refer exclusively to the letter of the text without considering the recipient to whom the text was addressed, along with the reception of the text by the Church. Moreover, it must also be said that one cannot separate "the Peter of faith from the faith of Peter":[45] they are one, and this is why the Church of Saint Peter in Rome offers to the universal Church, in the confession of Christ, a guarantee of unity of faith, always preserved faithfully and intact by the Roman Catholic Church.[46]

Nevertheless, to confirm the authenticity of Matthew's text, we can observe a strong link between the three main Petrine texts of the New Testament: Matthew 16:17–19, Luke 22:31–34, and John 21:15–19. The broader context uniting them is the mystery of the Passion and Death (as is apparent in Luke). The words are

---

[42] Cullman, 203.
[43] Cullman, 211.
[44] Cullman, 158–59.
[45] Gerhard Müller, *Der Papst: Sendung und Auftrag* (Freiburg: Verlag Herder, 2017), 198.
[46] Müller, *Der Papst*, 198.

said in view of the Passion and the Lord foretells Peter's denial but also his conversion in order that he may "confirm the brethren." The immediate context of Matthew's Gospel is the confession of Caesarea Philippi, where Peter declares his faith in Christ and receives in return the *munus* from the Lord, along with the keys to the Kingdom of heaven. At first glance, it seems that Matthew is reordering the Petrine event. And yet, in Matthew too, through Peter's confession, we are pointed forward to the mystery of the Lord's Passion and Death: the first prophecy of it by Jesus is followed by the terrible rebuke of the one who had just been exalted up to heaven through his power to bind and to loose; now suddenly Peter behaves like Satan. Peter's denial, which does not cause the loss of the primacy infallibly entrusted to him by Christ, will later be atoned for by his threefold profession of faith at the Sea of Galilee during the appearance of the Risen One. In his Gospel, John makes reference to the account of the Passion and Death, and with the teaching relating to the "flock," to the lambs and sheep, He echoes, through the account of the Last Supper, Matthew's doctrine that the "Church"—another name for the flock—is founded upon Peter.[47] Therefore, the Petrine ministry is not a late addition on the part of the community to which Matthew belonged, but a clear teaching of Jesus well-known to His apostles and disciples.

Peter as "rock" of the Church

We must now answer the following question: is the rock on which Christ builds His Church Peter, the person of the fisherman of

---

[47] Cullmann defends this unity of the three pericopes and therefore the authenticity in Matthew's Gospel of the words Jesus addressed to Peter; see, in particular, pp. 183–84 of his above-mentioned work.

Galilee, chosen as head of the apostolic college, or is it He Himself? At first glance, the answer to the question seems obvious for the reason that, if Christ chose Peter and stated that He would build His Church upon him, there appears to be no reason for seeing Christ Himself as the foundation. Yet, if we delve further, it becomes necessary to understand the nature of Peter's relationship with Christ. To eliminate Christ as the ultimate foundation would mean seeing the Church as a merely human structure built on man; to eliminate Peter would mean removing from it any visible consistency and transforming it into an invisible body without hierarchy and thus, without sacraments.

Among the patristic testimonies we can mention that of St. Cyprian, according to whom Christ designates Peter as the principle of unity of the Church, founded therefore on one single person.[48] Also, according to St. Leo the Great, Peter is the rock of the Church who, persevering with the firmness of stone, does not abandon the government of the Church.[49] This universal government, though later transferred to the person of Leo the Great (or whoever is in the office at the time), is the same as that of the Apostle Peter. Commemorating his coronation, Leo the Great writes: "For the sturdiness of that faith which was praised in the leader of the apostles endures. Just as what Peter believed in Christ remains, there likewise remains what Christ instituted in Peter."[50] Peter's faith is therefore the presupposition for his being constituted

---

[48] St. Cyprian, *De catholicæ Ecclesiæ unitatæ*, cc. 4–5.
[49] St. Leo the Great, *Sermo 3: De Natali ipsius; habitus in anniversario die assumptionis eiusdem ad summi pontificii munus*, c. 3.
[50] St. Leo the Great, *Sermo 3*, ch. 2, in *The Fathers of the Church*, vol. 93, trans. Jane Patricia Freeland, CSBJ and Agnes Josephine Conway, SSJ (Washington, DC: The Catholic University of America Press, 1996), 22.

as a rock. Origen, in a singular fashion, prefers to see in the "rock" a reference to every imitator of Christ who, with Peter, pronounces the words of faith in the divinity of the Logos.[51] Among all the testimonies of the Fathers, however, one by St. Augustine stands out in particular. In a text of the *Retractationes*, he seems undecided on which exegetical interpretation to prefer, that is, if the rock is Peter, his person, or instead Christ who builds Peter on Himself. "The reader may choose for himself which of the two opinions is more likely," says Augustine:

> Also at the time of my priestly ordination, I wrote a book *Against the Letter of Donatus*, who, after Majorinus, was the second bishop of the party of Donatus at Carthage. In this letter, he argues that the baptism of Christ is believed to be only in his communion. It is against this letter that we speak in this book. In a passage in this book, I said about the Apostle Peter, "On him as on a rock the Church was built." This idea is also expressed in song by the voice of many in the verses of the most blessed Ambrose where he says about the crowing of the cock: "At his crowing he, this rock of the Church, washed away his guilt."[52] But I know that very frequently at a later time,[53] I explained what the Lord said—"Thou art Peter, and upon this rock I will build my Church" (Mt 16:18)—so that it was understood as built upon Him whom Peter confessed saying: "Thou art the Christ, the Son of the living God" (cf. Mt 16:16; Jn 6:70), and so Peter, called after this rock, has received "the keys

---

51 Origen, *Commentaria in Evangelium secundum Matthæum*, XII, 22.23.

52 St. Ambrose, *Hymn.* 1; cf. *Exam.* 5, 24, 88.

53 See *Sermo* 76, 1, 1.

of the kingdom of heaven" (cf. Mt 16:19). For "Thou art Peter" and not "Thou art the rock" was said to him. But "the rock was Christ" (cf. 1 Cor 10:4), in confessing whom, as also the whole Church confesses, Simon was called Peter. But let the reader decide which of these two opinions is the more probable.[54]

Quite often, St. Augustine preferred Christ as the rock on which Peter himself rests. In *Sermon 76* on the Gospel of Matthew 14:24–33, he dwells at length on the meaning of "rock" and concludes that this rock can only be Christ. As he explains:

Therefore Peter is so called from the rock; not the rock from Peter; as Christ is not called Christ from the Christian, but the Christian from Christ. "Therefore," he saith, "Thou art Peter; and upon this Rock which thou hast confessed, upon this Rock which thou hast acknowledged, saying, 'Thou art the Christ, the Son of the living God, will I build my Church'; that is upon Myself, the Son of the living God, 'will I build My Church.' I will build thee upon Myself, not Myself upon thee."[55]

Further, to highlight the fact that the Church is founded on Christ and not on men, even if they were the apostles Peter and Paul—and indeed some brethren had been saying: "I belong to Paul," or "I belong to Apollos," or "I," on the contrary, "belong

54 *Retractationes, Contra epistulam Donati heretici liber unus*, 1, in *The Fathers of the Church*, vol. 60, trans. M. Inez Bogan, RSM (Washington, DC: The Catholic University of America Press, 1968), 90–91.

55 *Sermo 76*, 1, 1. English text of *Sermon 26*, 1 (76 Ben.) from Philip Schaff, ed., *Nicene and Post-Nicene Fathers* (Peabody, MA: Hendrickson, 1995), vol. 6, p. 340.

to Cephas," that is, "to Peter" (cf. 1 Cor 1:12)—Saint Augustine adds that "as no one was baptized in the name of Paul, so neither in the name of Peter, but all in the name of Christ; in this way Peter was built on stone, not the stone on Peter."[56] This second exegetical interpretation, if removed from the context of all of Saint Augustine's works, would favor Luther's vision.[57] The latter interprets the rock as Christ Himself and then draws the conclusion according to which the words addressed to Peter do not have in view his person, but only his faith in Jesus the Rock. In this hypothesis, the Church would not be founded on the rock of the Roman Church, but on the faith that Peter confesses for the entire Church. All Protestant reformers, in any case, agree on the fact that Peter was designated as a "rock" not insofar as he is a person, but rather as a believer.[58] According to Cullmann, however, this hypothesis is unsatisfactory, both due to the fact that the context in which Jesus addresses the words to Peter has little to do with Peter's faith—which was hardly exemplary—and the fact that the connection between the two declarations "You are Peter" (*kepha*) and "on this rock I will build my Church" explicitly indicates that the reference is to the person of the Apostle.[59] Yet even Cullmann's position, as we have seen, according to which the ministry as "rock" ends with the person of Peter, is unsatisfactory.

---

[56] *Sermo* 76, 2, 2.
[57] See references quoted by Cullmann, *Peter*, 162.
[58] See Cullman, 163.
[59] Agostino Trapè, "La 'Sedes Petri' in S. Agostino," in *Miscellanea Antonio Piolanti*, vol. II (Rome: Facultas Theologiæ Pontificiæ Universitatis Lateranensis, 1964), 1–19. See also Giuseppe Di Corrado, *Pietro pastore della Chiesa negli scritti di Agostino d'Ippona* (Roma: Città Nuova, 2012).

It is therefore advisable to clarify, with Fr. Agostino Trapè's scholarship, some solid conclusions that can be drawn from the writings of St Augustine: Jesus confers on Peter a primacy among the Apostles; Rome is the See of Peter; the succession of the bishops of Rome is a guarantee of the apostolicity of the Church; in the Church of Rome there is the principality of the Apostolic Chair, which exercises supreme and definitive doctrinal authority for the whole Church. Moreover, the Augustinian Father, analyzing the passages in which St. Augustine comments on the pericope under consideration in Matthew (16:18–19), concludes by saying that the two interpretations of "on this rock" have no bearing on St. Augustine's theological doctrine. Christ is certainly the rock and foundation of the Church, without which the Church would be built upon men, but this notion is extended in the pastors of the Church, who therefore also become "rock." The reality, on the part of the shepherds, of being "rock," is rooted in the relation between Christ and the Church, as represented by the shepherds. The Church realizes her essence as a rock by remaining faithful to Christ, the only Shepherd and original rock.

Hence, Peter becomes a rock in Christ and through Him; he is a mediator in Christ, not *principaliter et perfective* but *ministerialiter et dispositive*.[60] We can rightly say with Aquinas that Christ is a rock *in and of Himself*, while Peter is a rock insofar as he is a confessor of Christ and His representative. Christ in Himself is the foundation of the Church, but the Apostles are as well, according to the measure of Christ's gift and of the authority

---

[60] Not principally and perfectively, but ministerially and dispositively. See Müller, *Der Papst*, 205.

conferred on them in Christ.[61] Therefore it is difficult, if not impossible, to raise doubt biblically and systematically about Christ's will in relation to the visible faith and communal confession of the faith of His Church, which has in Peter the visible principle of its unity with God.[62] Peter's faith is the reason why he was constituted by Christ as the foundation of His Church.[63]

Thus, Peter is the "rock," but to be this, he must be subject to the Word of God. The Congregation for the Doctrine of the Faith in a note on the Petrine primacy expresses it thus:

> The Roman Pontiff—like all the faithful—is subject to the Word of God, to the Catholic faith, and is the guarantor of the Church's obedience; in this sense he is *servus servorum Dei*. He does not make arbitrary decisions, but is spokesman for the will of the Lord, who speaks to man in the Scriptures lived and interpreted by Tradition; in other words, the *episkope* of the primacy has limits set by divine law and by the Church's divine, inviolable constitution found in Revelation. The Successor of Peter is the rock which guarantees a rigorous fidelity to the Word of God against arbitrariness and conformism: hence the martyrological nature of his primacy.[64]

---

[61] St. Thomas Aquinas, *Super Matt.* on Mt 16:17, cited in Müller, *Der Papst*, 206.

[62] See Müller, *Der Papst*, 206.

[63] See Ludwig Ott, *Fundamentals of Catholic Dogma* (Cork: The Mercier Press, 1958), 281.

[64] Congregation for the Doctrine of the Faith, *The Primacy of the Successor of Peter in the Mystery of the Church*, no. 7, in *L'Osservatore Romano*, October 31, 1998, p. 7.

Peter, *persona credente*

Peter is the rock of the Church; his person has been made capable of exercising this ministry by Christ, of having faith in Him. Faith is united to the person and therefore we could speak of Peter, the pope, as a believing person. Faith is the reason for his being a rock, and the rock, which is his own person, is in turn based on faith in Christ and on the faith of the Church. The objective faith that recognizes Christ as the Son of God precedes the institution of the Petrine primacy, strengthens it, and manifests its finality. Peter—the pope—in the full line of his successors, from age to age, professes the same faith in Christ; insofar as he professes it, he sums up in his person the whole process of the development of the Faith's doctrine. In the faith of Peter and of his successors, therefore, the Tradition of the Church is manifested; conversely, the Tradition of the Church lives and manifests itself principally in the faith of the pope. If there were a contradiction between Peter's faith and the *traditio fidei*, this would mean that the pope's faith had distanced itself from the faith of the Church and that therefore it would be necessary and urgent for him to submit himself once again to this faith. However, it never means that the Church is obliged to submit itself to the subjective faith of such a pope. To put Peter's personal faith before the Faith of the Church is to sink into subjectivism and dogmatic relativism.

Hence there is a profound unity between the person of Peter and the faith of Peter. They are so united that they are no longer separable, unless a pope chooses to be unfaithful to his mission of being the rock, to renounce believing and thus to renounce confirming his brethren. It is Peter himself who, chosen by Christ, is founded on the immutable rock of the Faith and this rock is Christ alone. Christ founds the faith of Peter and therefore brings into being the person of the pope as the rock of the Church. In this manner Christ establishes the Church on a firm and unchanging foundation. Even if the faith of this or that pope were to fail, Peter's faith would never do so, as it is always a divine gift of interior illumination. When a pope renounces the exercise of his *munus* proper, which is confirming the brethren in the Faith, and even goes so far as teaching ambiguous doctrines verging on heresy, that does not immediately mean that that pope is not a true pope. Rather, we would need to ask how it is possible for the faith of a pope to fail. Although raised to the highest degree of dignity in the Church, with a grace proportionate to his state, he still remains Simon—someone who struggles to become Peter and lets himself be dazzled by various temptations, by the spirit of the age which from time to time proposes an easier way, a way that is not that of the Cross. Simon would prefer Jesus to refrain from going to Jerusalem to be crucified and to die, but is rebuked in no uncertain terms, because he had become like Satan, one who divides man from God (cf. Mt 16:21–23). Peter, on the other hand, once he repented, allows himself to be crucified like the Master. Concerning the entire episode of Capernaum (Mt 16:15–23), Ven. Fulton Sheen writes:

> Here in a vignette we have the entire paradox, which has proved for many a stumbling stone, a scandal, of infallibility and peccability. We have Christ's vicar divinely guided in his office as key-bearer to the gates of heaven and of earth. We also have this same Peter, the rock, the bearer of the keys, left to himself and without guidance, stigmatized as Satan. Paradox it is, but also a fact.... Peter was willing to confess Christ the priest, but not Christ the victim. Men called to be rocks can become stones of stumbling. The Lord himself, however, defined His terms of service in

clear language. The priesthood means imitation of Christ, and imitation means self-crucifixion.[65]

If the Faith grows dim or there is a crisis in the Church in its entirety, Simon Peter's faith will also be affected, and risk being swept away. If it happens that the Successor of Peter obeys the new dictates of a group that has been committed for years to changing the Faith in the name of ever-evolving and whimsical pastoral experiments, to make it more amenable to the world, then such a Peter, no longer being a teacher of truth and father of souls, and favoring an Antichristic path, would become, in the most extreme contradiction of what he is, an instrument of doctrinal confusion.[66] He would thus be the main enemy of the Church's faith. Yet even in these cases the love for the pope remains immutable because it is not based on personal sympathy or antipathy, but solely on his being "Peter who believes." If such a Peter falters in his faith, he is all the more in need of help on the part of the whole Church: all the more charity and all the more prayer. Thus, criticism addressed to the pope will not be calling into question his *munus*—unless there is clear evidence indicating this—but will only aim at verifying, in the light of the Church's perennial teaching, whether this *munus* is being exercised or not, that is, whether the Petrine role is being fulfilled or not, whether the faith and morals being taught by the pope are the faith and morals of the Church.

When Jesus declares Peter blessed for having correctly professed faith in His divinity, He also highlights the fact that that faith was not revealed to him by flesh or blood. In other words,

---

[65] Fulton Sheen, *The Priest Is Not His Own* (London: Peter Davies, 1963), 143–44.

[66] See Julia Meloni, *The St. Gallen Mafia: Exposing the Secret Reformist Group Within the Church* (Gastonia, NC: TAN Books, 2021).

it is not the fruit of his human ability, but revealed by the Father who is in heaven (cf. Mt 16:17). This supposes that there could be a pseudo-faith or an erroneous teaching stemming from the flesh and blood of Peter, that is, from that material and this-worldly man that Peter still remains. This can be seen, for example, in Peter's duplicitous behavior, when he ate with the pagans and then kept himself apart from them out of fear of the circumcised (cf. Gal 2:11–14). Paul had to correct him publicly. If he had not, this ambiguous pastoral behavior, based on a doctrinal ambiguity about the *Torah*'s role as it related to faith in Christ, which operates by means of charity, would have led to two Christian communities being created: one comprised of the pagans and the other, more orthodox, of converts from Judaism. Peter would thus have been the cause of scandal and schism in the Church. But Paul justly opposes him openly (cf. Gal 2:11).[67] Rare are those in our day who, like Paul, have the courage and determination to do likewise in similar circumstances.

---

[67] St. Thomas Aquinas writes: "It must be observed that, if there is a proximate danger to the faith, prelates must be rebuked, even publicly, by their subjects. Thus St. Paul, who was subject to St. Peter, rebuked him publicly, because of an imminent danger of scandal in matters of faith. And, as St Augustine says in his commentary, 'St Peter himself gave an example to those who govern, so that they, sometimes straying from the right path, would not reject as undue a correction that came even from their subjects' (*ad Gal.* 2:14)" (*Summa theologiæ* II-II, q. 33, a. 4, ad 2). In accord with this teaching of the Angelic Doctor, a large group of theologians and scholars published and signed the *Correctio filialis de hæresibus propagatis* to denounce the heresies that risk being favored because of the equivocal teachings of Pope Francis. For the text and accompanying and related documents, see John R.T. Lamont and Claudio Pierantoni, *Defending the Faith against Present Heresies* (Waterloo, ON: Arouca Press, n.d.).

Faith, the most precious good the Church possesses, does not come from flesh and blood, but from God. It is an act of obedience to God and to its uninterrupted transmission in the Church, through the Church's obedience to the Faith as transmitted. If it should happen, however, that the notion of *traditio fidei* is lost and the Tradition of the Church comes to be considered as a sort of historical archive and no longer as the *regula fidei*, even the pope's faith would be lost. He would no longer understand its origin and therefore its purpose. Hence, it would easily come to be dictated to him by flesh and blood.

Peter's act of "confirming the brethren" in the Faith also comes after his being "converted" (*pote epistrépsas*, cf. Lk 22:31–32), that is, after turning anew toward Christ, or after returning to the true faith for which Jesus Himself prays, so that it may not be eclipsed (*eklípse*) in the person of Peter. Let us say it once again: it is not Peter who founds the faith of the Church, but, on the contrary, it is the Faith that founds Peter and his *munus* proper, namely, to teach the Faith and therefore to confirm his brethren. The Faith founds Peter as a believing person and thus builds up the Church, a believing body. In this sense, every pope in the Church must always be a suprapersonal figure of the one Peter who believes and who is blessed for his faith.

Munus petrinum and infallible magisterium according to *Pastor Æternus*

It is a dogma of faith that the primacy of jurisdiction of St. Peter continues in the Church through his successors. The First Vatican Council with *Pastor Æternus* defined the *munus petrinum* of the Roman Pontiff, establishing the causes and limits of his infallibility.[68]

---

[68] DH 3050–75.

This dogmatic constitution recognizes the essence of this primacy in a twofold unity: so that the Episcopate might be one and undivided, and so that the whole multitude of believers might be preserved in the unity of faith and communion. This primacy of jurisdiction over the whole Church was promised and conferred by Christ, immediately and directly, on the Apostle Peter. In fact, Simon, to whom the Lord had already addressed the words "you shall be called Cephas" (Jn 1:42), after he had pronounced his confession of faith was constituted the stone of the Church, and to him Christ entrusted the keys of the kingdom of heaven (cf. Mt 16:16–19). To Simon Peter alone, after His resurrection, Jesus conferred the authority of supreme shepherd and guide of the whole flock with the words: "Feed my lambs ... feed my sheep" (Jn 21:15–17). *Pastor Æternus* establishes, in addition to this, that it is to be believed by divine and Catholic faith that whoever succeeds Peter to the same chair, by virtue of the institution of Christ Himself, obtains the primacy of Peter over the whole Church.[69]

Furthermore, Vatican I confirms, by virtue of the constant tradition of the Church and the declarations of the Ecumenical Councils (especially those celebrated in the East in agreement with the West), that the Holy See has always held that, in the same Apostolic primacy of the Roman Pontiff as successor of Peter, Prince of all the Apostles, is also contained the supreme *munus* of magisterium. Nonetheless, this *munus* is not unlimited. *Pastor Æternus* sets precise limits when it teaches:

> For the Holy Spirit was promised to the successors of Peter not so that they might, by his revelation, make known some new doctrine, but that, by his assistance, they might

[69] DH 3057.

religiously guard and faithfully expound the revelation or deposit of faith transmitted by the apostles.[70]

In Chapter IV, after outlining the doctrine concerning the infallible magisterium of the pope, *Pastor Æternus* formulates the definition of his infallibility. Infallibility is *not* impeccability or personal indefectibility on the part of the pope, but only the ability to teach without any error and with absolute certainty when the pontiff speaks *ex cathedra*, that is, solemnly as pastor and doctor of all Christians and with the intention of defining a doctrine of faith or morals. This infallibility is what the Divine Redeemer wanted His Church to be equipped with. The whole Church is bound by such teaching; its irreformability stems from itself, not from the consent of the Church.[71] In this way, and particularly thanks to the "*non autem ex consensus ecclesiæ*," Pius IX intended to expunge the final attempt of the minority of the Fathers at Vatican I to make the Roman Pontiff's infallibility depend on that of the Church, and to be able to greatly limit the text of the definition, since it had not been possible to prevent it.[72] No doubt it was a Gallican remnant, which was thereby definitively defeated.[73]

There was the well-known incident during the council initiated by the Dominican Filippo Maria Guidi, created cardinal by Pius IX in 1863, which had rekindled the hopes of this minority.[74] In his speech in the conciliar hall he wondered if papal infallibility

---

[70] DH 3070.

[71] DH 3074.

[72] See John W. O'Malley, *Vatican I: The Council and the Making of the Ultramontane Church* (Cambridge, MA: The Belknap Press, 2018), 208–9.

[73] See Philippe Chenaux, "Il primato petrino nel contesto del Vaticano I," in *Lateranum* 87, no. 1 (2021): 21.

[74] See O'Malley, *Vatican I*, 210–14.

was personal and if it was separate from the Church. He argued that such infallibility does not make the person of the pope infallible as if it were a personal quality. Divine assistance was not promised to the *person* but to the *acts* of the pope: it is the act that is infallible. Moreover, the pope did not depend on the bishops for the ability to issue an infallible judgment, but, in Guidi's judgment, he had to learn from the bishops the *sensus* of the Church on a given question. The pope had to consult the bishops and only after such consultation could he act. Guidi suggested changing the title of Chapter IV of *Pastor Æternus* to "The infallibility of the Roman Pontiff in the definition of dogmas."

The deputation of the council adopted a title very close to Guidi's suggestion, but proposed as such by Bishop Martin: *De Romani Pontifice Infallibili Magisterio*. The classical expression *ex cathedra* was also inserted to clarify that not all the teachings of the pope are infallible, but only those which are clearly indicated as such and are solemnly proclaimed.[75] Bishop Vinzenz Gasser of Brixen was entrusted with the task of presenting the text in the hall before the vote on Chapter IV.[76] The latter specified that papal infallibility was *personal* insofar as it belongs to the pontiff as the legitimate successor of Peter and only to the extent that he acts as a *public* person, that is, as head of the Church and in relation to it. Papal infallibility was *separated* from that of the Church by the special assistance of the Holy Spirit given to Peter according to the words of Jesus in Luke's Gospel (22:32). Gasser then highlighted the fact that the pope is infallible only when he speaks as pastor representing the universal Church (*universalem ecclesiam ræpresentans*). The pontiff is not separated from the rest of

[75] See O'Malley, 215.
[76] See O'Malley, 216–17.

the Church, but prior consent or subsequent confirmation could never be a condition for an infallible pronouncement. Moreover, papal infallibility, it was specified, is not *absolute*, since only God is infallible absolutely. It can be such only within the limits set by Christ. Finally, Gasser stated that for *ex cathedra* infallibility to be such, it is necessary for the pope to make explicit his intention to define a doctrine. Infallibility is also promised to the episcopal body when it exercises the supreme magisterium with the Successor of Peter.[77] The clarifications and amendments presented by the Bishop of Brixen were very precise and placed the pope and the Church in a correct relationship. However, they did not convince the minority who, having been defeated, preferred to leave the council before the final vote.[78]

In this way, infallibility was put into its proper framework, correcting the erroneous intent to subordinate papal infallibility to the Church; it also corrected the error that we could call an excess in the opposite direction, consisting of the wish to see, as is common in our day, an infallibility in all the interventions of the pope, even in his every word. There are definitely two other manifestations of infallibility in the magisterium of the Roman Pontiff and of the bishops in communion with him: the reiteration of an ordinary magisterium already taught by other popes or councils, or the declaration of the definitiveness of a teaching of the ordinary magisterium, even if it does not arrive at a dogmatic definition of this doctrine.[79] Both these modes of infallibility are seamlessly linked to *ex cathedra* infallibility, inasmuch as they

---

[77] See Mansi 52:1213BC–1214A; *Lumen Gentium* 25.

[78] See O'Malley, *Vatican I*, 220.

[79] See CIC can. 750, §1 and §2; *Professio fidei et Iusiurandum fidelitatis*, in *AAS* 81 (1989): 104f.

attest to the necessity of apostolic Tradition for a doctrine to be reiterated by the magisterium or to be held definitively so as to safeguard the deposit of faith or to better explain it. An infallible definition always refers to the apostolic Tradition,[80] which is the ultimate object of the infallibility of a doctrine revealed by God and made explicit by its uninterrupted transmission in the Church. This is yet another reason for acknowledging that not every teaching of the pope is infallible, but only those which flow from the Church's constant Tradition.

Precisely in reference to this, the Instruction *Donum Veritatis*, "On the ecclesial vocation of the theologian," when distinguishing the various levels of the magisterium, specifies that theologians may intervene in open questions, those that are still under debate, in which, along with solid principles, contingent and merely speculative issues are also involved. These are interventions of a "prudential order," and have already been known to have shortcomings.[81] The pope's ordinary magisterium may contain errors due to human imprudence, often caused by the desire to find a hasty solution to changing situations. Therefore, to view the pope's infallibility as entailing a continual guarantee of the truth of his words—a sort of unlimited divine approbation or, as happens today, a proof of his valid election—is far from what Petrine infallibility means and therefore from what the pope is. In the final analysis, that is to confuse infallibility with authority (from *auctoritas*, authorization) and to make the latter depend on the former, when in fact infallibility depends on authority. Authority does not emerge from infallibility but from the election of a pope to the papal throne.

---

[80]   Cf DH 3074.

[81]   See Congregation for the Doctrine of Faith, Instruction *Donum Veritatis*, May 24, 1990, no. 24; *AAS* 82 (1990): 1560.

The pope and the Church

The pope's office is confirming the Faith, not fashioning or abolishing it according to his whims. In this sense, the Church's faith revealed by God precedes the person of the pope. He is responsible for confirming it, exposing errors against it, and teaching it definitively and infallibly. The rule of our faith is the doctrine of the Church according to its constant transmission (*"tradidi enim vobis in primis quod et accipi,"* 1 Cor 15:3); the one who "confirms" this rule and offers the faithful the norm of true belief is the Roman Pontiff. Jesus said to Peter: "Simon, Simon, behold, Satan has asked to have you, that he might sift you like wheat, but I have prayed for you that your faith may not fail; and when you have turned again, strengthen your brethren" (Lk 22:31–32). Peter must believe *with* the whole Church; he must profess his faith correctly so that he can confirm others in that same faith. Faith is above the pope and is therefore the only thing capable of judging him. In one of his sermons, Innocent III expounded this very important doctrine: faith is so necessary to the pope that, while for all his sins God alone is his judge, for sins committed against the Faith, he can be judged by the Church.[82] This principle can already be found in the *Decretum Gratiani*, where there is an assertion attributed to St. Boniface (bishop of Mainz and quoted by Ivo of Chartres),[83] according to which the pope *can* err in the Faith, therefore he cannot be judged by anyone except when he deviates from the

---

[82] *"In tantum fides mihi necessaria est ut cum de ceteris peccatis solum Deum judicem habeam, propter solum peccatum quod in fidem committitur possem ab Ecclesia judicari"*: Innocent III, Sermo II, In consacratione Pontificis Maximi, *PL* 217:656.

[83] Ivo of Chartres, *Decretales*, pars V, c. 23, *PL* 161:330.

Faith.[84] Canon 1404 of the CIC, which reads *"prima sedes a nemine judicatur"* underlines the injudicability of the Roman Pontiff as supreme legislator.[85] He who makes the law is not judged by the law. This is canon law, above which, nevertheless, there is the immutability of the Church's faith as received and transmitted. The law is made in accordance with the faith of the Church and for the sake of protecting this faith. Just as the Code of Canon Law depends on divine Revelation, so the pope depends on the faith emanating from divine Revelation itself. It follows that the "Bishop of Rome who leads the first See as Successor of Peter is not above the Gospel or the Church. Nor can Peter's Office be understood by analogy to an absolutist czar or dictator."[86]

But what if a pope does not believe, or ceases to believe? Would he still be pope? A pope might lose the Faith or go through a profound trial like that of the first Peter (cf. Lk 22:32), which would lead him to deny the Lord. However, this would not mean that he would *ipso facto* lose his *munus petrinum*, nor would it constitute a clear sign of the real absence of the *munus*. By loss of faith we mean the objective *fides quæ* according to the canon of the Church, i.e., the public confession of Christ according to Scripture and Tradition; we do not mean the *fides qua* which could still be given as a subjective act. An absence of faith could be deduced from the actions, facts, and equivocal documents that could ride the tide of

---

[84] *"Huius [scil., papæ] culpas redarguere præsumit mortalium nullus, quia cunctos ipse judicaturus a nemine est judicandus, nisi deprehendatur a fide devius."* Anonymous, *Decretum*, pars I, d. 40, c. 6, *PL* 107:215.

[85] A principle sanctioned by Vatican I (cf. DH 3063) and formulated juridically by the CIC of 1917, can. 1556.

[86] Weigel, *The Next Pope*, 42.

heresy, though always veiled, never fully embraced or made explicit. This could be the biggest hazard to evaluate, even before considering the hypothesis of a heretical pope.[87] The problem that grips the Church today is not only (or not so much) heresy, material or formal, but a broader and more widespread open mistrust with regard to the Faith as such, which instead could be characterized as apostasy. It is difficult to deny that features of a *de facto* apostasy are emerging in our day, due to the fact that blatant and gross

[87] On the hypothesis of a heretical pope, see the essay by Arnaldo Xavier da Silveira, *Can a Pope Be . . . a Heretic? The Theological Hypothesis of a Heretical Pope*, in *Two Timely Issues: The New Mass and the Possibility of a Heretical Pope*, trans. John Russell Spann and José Aloisio Schelini (Spring Grove, PA: The Foundation for a Christian Civilization, 2022). In addition to gathering theological opinions on the subject, Silveira also offers his position that begins with the hypothesis of St. Robert Bellarmine: the heresy of a pope should be known *to the entire Church*; no authority on earth can depose the pope, but the heretical pope would depose himself. This, naturally, would prevent the pope from exercising his jurisdiction. Contrary to the theological hypothesis presented by Silveria is the opinion of Bishop Athanasius Schneider in his essay "On the Question of a Heretical Pope," published at the *OnePeterFive* website on March 20, 2019. In it, the Auxiliary Bishop of Astana argues that the hypothesis of the deposition of a heretical pope is untenable and would in any case open the way, in some sense, to sedevacantism and to conciliarism. The most certain guarantee of the inapplicability of the deposition of a heretical pope is the Tradition of the Church, which has never taught that a pope can be legitimately deposed. Bishop Schneider has revisited this topic a number of times: see, e.g., "On the question of the true pope in the light of the opinion of the automatic loss of the papal office for heresy and the speculations about the resignation of Benedict XVI," *OnePeterFive*, February 28, 2020; "On the Validity of Pope Francis," *OnePeterFive*, September 19, 2023.

errors are being spread far and wide, without anyone in authority correcting them openly, and indeed these are often favored by the hierarchy and local Churches.[88] Those who are silent simply to avoid scandalizing the faithful or to avoid causing comments indicating division among pastors unfortunately do not render a service to the Gospel. Instead, they allow error to suffocate the truth and faith to be extinguished. For a heresy to be such, it is necessary that its presence be recognizable by the Church, that is, that it be *manifest*.[89] But how can we detect a heresy if in some way the problem is the entire ecclesial climate—one clouded by the presence of a more generalized or, rather, "liquid" apostasy?[90] This is why errors concerning faith are no longer recognized as such, but have even become out-and-out programs of action and commonplace pastoral proposals.

---

[88] See Weigel, *The Next Pope*, 50. The author here highlights what the next pope is called to do by reflecting on the situation created with Pope Francis, with "wayward local Churches" placed "into *de facto* states of apostasy or schism." Nothing has come yet from Rome to condemn the schismatic approval by the German Synod of blessings for same-sex couples, the discussion of female diaconate, and the inclusion of LGBT people without asking for a change in their way of living. This *de facto* schismatic decision by a large majority of German Bishops came on March 10, 2023 (see www.synodalerweg.de).

[89] The notoriety and dissemination of the heresy are also necessary for a heretical pope to be considered as deposed due to the same heresy (cf. Silveira), or in any case deposable. In a more subtle way, "theologians debate whether the loss of the pontificate occurs at the moment in which he falls into heresy or only in the case that heresy becomes manifest or notorious and publicly disseminated": see de Mattei, *Vicario di Cristo*, 124, with reference to Salaverri, *De Ecclesia Christi*, in *Sacra Theologiæ Summa* (Madrid: B.A.C., 1958), vol. 1, pp. 881–82.

[90] See chapter 2.

That the pope can fall into heresy, then, is the most commonly asserted opinion among theologians and canonists.[91] A pope might lapse into heresy when he is not exercising the fullness of his authority, that is, his office as universal pastor and doctor, allotting his teaching to the lowest degree of authentic ordinary magisterium (which, as we said, may contain errors). Still, he could never define, in the fullness of his magisterial authority, a heretical doctrine: he is prevented from doing so by the dogma of Petrine infallibility. Such a thing would constitute a contradiction in terms.[92] Heresy is the obstinate denial of a doctrine of

---

[91] In the twelfth and thirteenth centuries all canonists knew and commented on the above-mentioned text of Gratian, and all admit without difficulty that the pope may fall into heresy as well as into all other mortal sins. Their only preoccupation is how, in that case, he can be judged by the Church. In the fifteenth century the same doctrine still exists among numerous authors, including Card. Torquemada (*Summa de Ecclesia* lib. 2, c. 112 [Rome, 1469]), according to which, in case of heresy, either the pope immediately loses the papal dignity or is deposed by the fact itself. Only one exception occurs, namely, with the Dutch theologian Alberto Pighi (*Hierarchiæ ecclesiasticæ assertio*, lib. 4, c. 8 [Cologne, 1538], fol. 131ff.), according to whom, owing to the promise of Our Lord to Peter (Mt. 16:18), it is *impossible* for the pope to be a heretic, because in that case the foundation of the Church would be threatened and it would be equivalent to affirming that the gates of hell had prevailed. In this viewpoint, Pighi was opposed by Melchior Cano. For an overview, see E. Dublanchy, "Infallibilité du pape," *Dictionnarie de théologie catholique*, t. 7, par. 2 (Paris: Letouzey et Ané, 1927), 1714–17; Roberto de Mattei, Foreword to Silveira's *Can a Pope Be...a Heretic?*, in idem, *Two Timely Issues*, 155–62.

[92] The Dominican Father Roger-Thomas Calmel (1914–1975) wrote in the late 1970s: "Since Jesus returned to Heaven, he has chosen and procured 263 popes. Some, only a small number, have been Vicars so faithful that we invoke them as friends of God

faith or of morals to be held with divine and Catholic faith, or obstinate doubt about it.[93] Obstinacy is an essential element of heresy, otherwise an error is being made, even a serious one, but it cannot be qualified as heresy, which would produce the loss of the Petrine office. However, whether a pope has lapsed into open heresy, or confined himself to a controversial, equivocal teaching, always on the verge of uncertainty and confusion, the underlying problem is the faith of Peter, of that pope. Therefore, a faith that is true, certain, and correct has as its measure the faith of the Church in its entirety and not the subjective faith of this or that pope.

There is no Church without the pope, but neither is there the pope without the Church. The two realities, as we said, are intrinsically united through a hierarchy that always has at its core and above all else, Christ and the faith in Him, as professed and transmitted uninterruptedly by the *traditio apostolica*. Peter and the Church always go together, but the Church is greater than

---

and holy intercessors; an even smaller number has fallen into very serious shortcomings; the greater number of the Vicars of Christ, on the other hand, were more or less suitable; none of them, being still pope, has betrayed and will be able to betray to the point of explicitly teaching heresy in the fullness of his authority . . .. And the most surprising is also that popes, who suffered cruel torments, for example a Pius VI or a Pius VII, were not declared saints either by the *vox ecclesiæ* or by the *vox populi*. If these popes, who suffered so much as popes, did not bear their pain with such a degree of love as to be canonized, how can we be surprised that other popes, who have embraced their office with a worldly mentality, can commit grave faults or impose on the Church of Christ a particularly terrible and heartbreaking trial?" *Breve Apologia della Chiesa di sempre* (Albano Laziale: Ichthys, 2007), 111; 120.

[93] See CIC, can. 751.

Peter: the former is the finality and the *raison d'être* of the latter, the place where he preserves firmness and consistency.

The relationship between the Petrine principle and the Marian principle of the Church can also help us in this consideration. Peter with his faith, as Balthasar explains, always stands before the Church as a "subjective spirit," which can never rise to the level of the objective spirit of primacy and of sacrament, both because Peter is a sinner, and in Christ alone, in His person, can the mission of mediator and redeemer coincide. Christ alone is priest and victim; He alone can unite, through the gift of self, the necessity of adoration and expiation, which are inherent to the priestly ministry. On the other hand, the Virgin Mary stands before the Church as an "objective spirit." Mary's faith is a personal response to the gift of the Bridegroom. Mary's *Fiat* is a response full of love, showing the immaculate fidelity of the Bride-Church on earth and preparing her most perfect fulfilment in heaven. Mary's faith alone is coextensive with the masculine principle of the Church, of the ministry and of the sacraments, though the latter can never fully encompass the former.[94] Thus the Virgin Mary believes as the Church and for the Church. If Peter's faith were to fail, Mary's faith would never fail. It seems that the situation of the Church today is that of Holy Saturday, when the complete faith of the Church is concentrated in the heart of Mary, in the One who gathered the whole Church around her *Fiat*. Mary believes and with her faith sustains the absent or wavering faith of the apostles.

The Church continues despite a pope's infidelity. When one pope dies—as the saying goes—another one is made; the Church

---

[94] See Hans Urs von Balthasar, "Who is the Church?," in *Explorations in Theology*, vol. II: *Spouse of the Word* (San Francisco: Ignatius Press, 1991), 161.

does not die at the death of the pope. In the interim of the choice of a successor, the Church remains firm, and it is the Church which welcomes the new pope. This interim's finality, however, is the election of the pope and its duration is not unlimited. The pope is therefore dependent upon the Church and not the contrary. This will always be the source of the hope that the Church will rise up even when there is a pope who is more obedient to the *Zeitgeist* than to Christ. The Church can never fail even if a pope acts against it by teaching worldly doctrines, the fruit of his intellect unenlightened by grace. In that case it would be his faith that is wavering, not the faith of Peter, which is a gift from the Father. Faith therefore judges Peter, and the holy faith alone. In this sense, when the Church remains united as a believing body, the union of all the members with their Head in the one *sensus fidei* is superior to Peter and judges a Peter lost in the meanderings of human and worldly thought. The infallibility *in credendo* of the Church precedes the infallibility *in docendo*. In such a case, even the humblest baptized person who professes the Symbol of Faith, would be authorized to rise up and correct the miscreant pope. The view is currently fashionable that the pope's infallibility (*ex cathedra*) would prevent the person of Peter from losing the Faith or from falling into doctrinal or moral errors. However, this is akin to saying that faith is the property of the pope or that it is the pope who makes the Faith. The Faith, instead, precedes Peter and only in this way infallibly establishes the Church. A pope who became a heretic in a formal way would contradict his Petrine ministry, but this would not mean that the Church would fail, since the gates of hell have no power against it. Furthermore, the pope who became a heretic would not demonstrate that he is not a true pope, but only that he is a pope without the faith of the Church, one with a human faith in a heretical doctrine—just as Judas's betrayal of his ministry does not mean that he was not a true apostle, or as Peter's denial of the Lord at the culminating moment when he should have borne witness to Him does not mean he lost the *munus* to confirm his brethren. These lapses prove only that Judas and Peter, in different ways, were unfaithful to the grace of their ministry.

If the pope failed in his office to confirm his brothers in the Faith, who would substitute for him? Certainly, the Church is not abandoned in this case. There is a Pontiff without blemish, Jesus Christ, "the great Shepherd of the sheep" (Heb 13:20). He is always present in His Church, and it is He who always remains faithful even if the one chosen as His vicar proves unfaithful to his task or is deemed unfit. The pope is the vicar of Christ, not Christ Himself. It is interesting in this regard to recall the circular letter of the Chancellor of Germany, Otto von Bismarck, after the proclamation of Petrine infallibility. The letter was written on May 14, 1872, and published on December 14, 1874. The main accusation raised, certainly subservient to the plan of the *Kulturkampf* to subject the German Church to the authority of the Empire, was that papal jurisdiction had now absorbed episcopal jurisdiction. The German bishops responded with a collective declaration in February 1875, later praised by Pius IX.[95] In it the bishops remind the Chancellor that the *potestas suprema, ordinaria et immediata* was conferred on the pope by Jesus Christ Himself in the person

---

[95] The Chancellor's letter was published in the *Deutschen Reichsanzeiger und Königlich Preussischen Staatsanzeiger* and reported in its main features by the bishops' response (DH 3112–17). Pius IX responded with the letter *Mirabilis Illa Constantia* to the Bishops of Germany, March 4, 1875 (DH 3117). For quotations and commentary, see Peter Kwasniewski, "Objections and Replies on 'Pastor Æternus,'" *OnePeterFive*, May 10, 2023.

of St. Peter, clearing the field of any possible confusion of this *potestas* with the monarchical power of the pontiff. In fact, the pope is not given "absolute power" any more than any monarch on earth. The Petrine primacy is exercised within the limits of ecclesiastical authority and is at the same time subject to divine law and bound by the directives given by Christ to the Church. The pope cannot change the constitution of the Church given to it by its divine Founder, though a ruler of this world can change the constitution of a State. The constitution of the Church is not subject to human arbitrariness. Moreover, the pope's power does not absorb that of the bishops due to the fact that both the papacy and the episcopate are of divine institution. The pope is given neither the right nor the power to change the rights and duties of the episcopate. Finally, to define the pope as "absolute sovereign" because of his infallibility is false. The bishops reminded Bismarck (and us today) that infallibility is a characteristic of the papacy, which refers *exclusively* to the supreme magisterium of the pope: it is coextensive with the scope of the infallible magisterium of the Church in general and is restricted to the contents of Sacred Scripture and Tradition, and to dogmas already defined previously by the magisterial authority of the Church.

Christ is watching over us, despite the worldly disorientation of a pope, and there is also His Church which, as regards the divine will of institution, precedes the words of Jesus addressed to Peter which conferred the latter's primacy. Jesus institutes His Church in several stages,[96] beginning with the gathering of the

---

[96] See Brunero Gherardini, *La Chiesa: mistero e servizio* (Rome: EDUSC, 1994); Benedict XVI, *The Origins of the Church: The Apostles and Their Co-Workers* (San Francisco: Ignatius Press, 2010).

Twelve of which Peter is the head (cf. Mk 3:13–19). This institution undergoes a solemn and visible moment in Jesus's words to Peter, and therefore in the conferral of the primacy to bind and loose (cf. Mt 16:18–19). The institution's most central moment occurs in the institution of the Most Holy Eucharist, when Jesus commands His followers: "Do this in memory of me" (Lk 22:19). Unquestionably, the sacramental institution of the Holy Sacrifice of Calvary, revealed in the divine Eucharist, is the most important ecclesiological moment, to the extent that we can say that it is the Eucharist that makes the Church. Henri de Lubac says that:

> If the sacrifice is accepted by God, and the Church's prayer listened to, this is because the Eucharist, in its turn, *makes the Church*, in the strict sense of the word. It is the sacrament, St Augustine tells us, *quo in hoc tempore consociatur Ecclesia* . . .[97]

Finally, at Pentecost the already constituted Church is manifested to all peoples. The gift of tongues (*polilalia*)—the ability to be understood by all nations gathered in Jerusalem (Acts 2:1–13)—represents the universal nature of the Church. Therefore, the Church does not begin with Peter, but with Christ and with His will to build it on Peter as a mystical, visible, and hierarchical body. All these moments of institution contribute to the constitution of the one Church. Hence, just as they are indivisibly bound with one another, so the papacy is indivisible with respect to the mystery-Church: there is no Church without the papacy and vice versa.

---

[97] Henri de Lubac, *The Splendour of the Church* (London: Sheed and Ward, 1956), 152, citing St Augustine, *Contra Faustum*, lib. 12, c. 20. The concept of the Eucharist that makes the Church was taken up by John Paul II in the encyclical *Ecclesia de Eucharistia* of April 17, 2003.

However, this mystery-Church is always greater with respect to the conferral of primacy on Peter, by reason of the sacraments, *in primis* of the Eucharist, of the Word of God, and of the Faith itself. Therefore, the Church will not come to an end because of Peter, that is, because of the infidelity of a pope, but will last until the final coming of Christ (cf. Mt 16:18). Finally, with the Church that watches over us, there is the faith of the Virgin Mary. It is Mary's faith that sustains the faith of the Church: despite the deep sleep or even open betrayal of her pastors and of Peter in particular, the Church in Mary and for Mary always continues to believe indefectibly. The precedence of Christ over the Church is therefore the precedence of the Church with respect to Peter, as regards the person of a single pontiff.

Conclusion

At the end of this chapter, we wish to summarize the main assumptions and the conclusions reached. Peter is the Rock of the Church, that is, the one who with his person, chosen by Christ, serves as the foundation for the building up of the Church. To be this and to remain a "rock" despite the waves and calamities to which Christ's ship is subject, he must be subject to the Word of God; he must remain faithful to that faith which he professes insofar as he is illumined interiorly by the Holy Spirit. The faith is a gift of Christ to Peter, so that the latter, by believing, will confirm his brethren. Only by believing with the Church and with her uninterrupted *traditio* can he confirm his brethren. The faith precedes Peter, just as Christ precedes the Church. The Church, the believing Body, united to its divine Head by virtue of the Holy Spirit, always therefore precedes the person of Peter—and every other bishop who succeeds the Fisherman of Galilee—not only chronologically but also ontologically. For Peter to be a rock for the Church and not a stumbling block, it is therefore necessary that he be a *persona credente*. If the Faith is the reason for his being a rock, the rock, which is himself, must be founded in turn on faith in Christ and on the faith of the Church.

If Peter decides not to believe with that faith which he receives as a gift, he will not be able to confirm his brethren. Yet he will not, for that reason, lose his office. This is the greatest mystery to be reckoned with. A man could be pope because he was elected to fill this office, without actually being that for which he was chosen. Such a situation would surely provoke unprecedented doctrinal confusion, causing a disbanding due to the absence of a sure guide and the obfuscation of the office of unity to which Peter is called. It would be a sort of Holy Saturday of the absence of Christ, where, however, faith does not vacillate because it is all in the Heart of Mary, the Heart of the one who believes in an immaculate manner as the Church-Spouse and thus sustains the Church in her darkest moments.

Finally, it is profoundly misguided to make the pope an oracle, confusing his infallibility, delimited by precise theological boundaries, with his authority. If the pope has authority by reason of his Petrine office, this does not imply that he is also always and automatically infallible. Indeed, there are situations that likewise raise serious doubts about the authoritativeness of his words, when, for example, his speech is more political than theological, even if it is difficult to distinguish the political from the theological. The same authority is weakened when the pope improvises speeches and states opinions like any other opinion-maker. Speaking much (a typical pastoral turning-point of the postconciliar magisterium?), which does not free us from erring (cf. Prov 10:19), has been a characteristic trait of the pope's dialogue for several years now. It begins with television interviews, book-length interviews, and books written by the pope, and reaches its peak in high-altitude meetings with journalists during papal journeys. Must the pope speak all the time, off-the-cuff, and in situations like those in which, asked to interpret the uproar of breaking news, he risks exposing himself as ignorant, partial, indiscreet, inadequate, even contradicted by the facts? If the pope is not infallible every time he speaks, and if most of the time he does not speak in conformity with the faith of the Church, this very fact does not mean that he is not the pope, that his election is not valid. It is a sign, rather, that his faith is not ecclesial. The invalidity of the election does not depend on the quality of his teaching, but on factors that would invalidate the elective process. These factors, to be such, must be evident not simply to some one person, but to the entire Church.

For the pope to really be what he is, he must believe in what he is. In a certain way, he is a mystery unto himself, which requires faith on his part, docility to God, and obedience to the uninterrupted Tradition of the Church. Recovering the concept of *traditio fidei* would also help to heal the very serious ecclesiological problems caused by its terrible *vacatio theologica* (theological absence).

2

Who Am I to Speak?

The present situation of the Church is truly appalling. An internal struggle being waged between truth and power is wearing her ragged. Truth means the Faith to be welcomed and safeguarded as received from Christ through the apostles; power, on the other hand, is the use of authority to change the Faith at all costs and adapt it according to the prevailing sentiments of the dominant culture. It seems that an echo of this struggle is manifest on the moral level in the antagonism between chastity and impurity; between the preservation of marriage and the priesthood for what they are and the imposition of libertinism and the desire to choose, instead, what is more convenient and easier. And the latter is justified with an appearance of doctrine.

Catholics are faced with a process of self-secularization that has been developing for several years now, but which is accelerating more than ever. It is the members of the Church themselves, even the highest authorities, who are contributing to the dissolution of Catholic identity for the sake of so-called "pastoral" purposes. Rather than efforts aimed at bringing back to Christ the millions of faithful who have distanced themselves from the Church and from the practice of the sacraments, instead a need is felt to give a new face to the Church, to free her from herself and from her past, and thus make her more fluid in her message, capable of adapting to all circumstances.

We are in the grip of a new form of Nominalism. Words are used to express something different from their original and genuine meaning. This is because they would not correspond to reality and would not express the truth of the matter we are discussing, but would be mere conventional signs to come to a social agreement. From this point of view, words and thoughts are mere illusions, and what matters is experience. When words, and thoughts, are commensurate with experience, that is, are experiential, then they manifest the truth. However, since experience is subjective and swiftly changes, words suffer the same fate. As with words, so with the concepts they try to express, obviously. Only yesterday, something was said that today is already no longer understandable or adaptable to the spirit of the age.

Specifically, one of the most nominalist words in current use is "pastoral." At one time it was understood as designating a "meal," a "pasture," which the shepherd provides for his flock. The sustenance given to the flock on the pasture was the Logos, the Truth. Then it became "pastoral science," whose role is to identify determining factors regarding the benefit or disadvantage of proposing any given doctrine, or of its proper formulation (this begins with the *praxis* to which the truth must adhere, but there is a risk of transforming the truth itself into *praxis*). Lately it has come to be conceived as a true and proper program of action understood as a "pastoral conversion" of the whole Church. This also has as its objective a "conversion of the papacy" and of the central structures of the Church, above all the organization of the Roman Curia.[98] Pastoral conversion then provides for an

---

[98] See Pope Francis, Apostolic Exhortation *Evangelii Gaudium*, no. 32.

"ecological conversion."[99] So what, now, does "pastoral" mean? Vatican II wished to avoid definitions and now we are immersed in a sort of theological do-it-yourself.

To recognize that we are sailing in nominalist waters, we can also refer to the case of the book written by the former Pope Benedict XVI and Cardinal Sarah. To the Vatican *entourage*, especially to the journalistic special forces that now serve as the theological bulwark of Santa Marta, what caused discomfort was not the book in defense of the priesthood and celibacy written by two eminent people, but the fact that, evidently, the previous pope stood in stark contrast with the current one. This would not have been beneficial for the image, already prevalent, of a Church divided between two popes. The problem was precisely that of the image of a weakened papacy and not the fact that the book defended and reiterated in an authoritative manner the reality of celibacy. The true motive for the dispute, which is celibacy, has been overlooked, but not without a precise reason. Since we are immersed in a new Nominalism, everyone is authorized to say what he thinks of celibacy (which no longer corresponds to any inherent truth, but is a *flatus vocis*, a meaningless word spoken in order to surpass celibacy and render it optional). However, no one is allowed to tarnish the (experience-based) media image that must be offered to the world. Experience, which in nominalist Empiricism serves as proof of the truth of concepts, now seems to be the exclusive prerogative of the media, something which they alone exercise. In the nominalist struggle, *what* is said is of little import; what counts is *how* it is said. Words thus become the vehicle of power; of the most appealing form of power, the ecclesiastical one, whose appeal stems from the fact that its authority

---

[99] See Pope Francis, Encyclical Letter, *Laudato Si'*, nos. 216–21.

is legitimized as a power come from God. It is justified by God: that is why this power is the most coveted, hence the many friends from the outside who seek to support it.

Faced with such a blatant decline of faith and plunged in a now unstoppable process of self-secularization, there are only a few who speak and defend the Faith. Why is this so? Before trying to identify the causes of this strange silence on the part of the Church's pastors, however, we need to specify what can or should be understood by "speaking." It is all the more fitting to do so, given the nominalist framework which surrounds this problem. In the age of social media and the global village, there is a demand that prelates speak and defend the Faith. This could be understood first and foremost—or perhaps exclusively—as an intervention on some website or through a *tweet*. While it is opportune and advantageous to use the media and social media in taking a stand in favor of the truth of the Faith, given the real time in which the fact is knowable by many and throughout the world, "speaking" implies much more. It means proclaiming the truth of the Gospel and defending it from the attacks of those who deny it. An apologetic element is needed. A faith left undefended from the assaults of error and slithering heresy easily becomes something other than itself: a new religion. If we have arrived at our present confusion, which no longer startles anyone, it is also because we have set aside the apologetic aspect of the Gospel proclamation. This proclamation or preaching of the divine Message—which may make use of mass media but which does not become mere communication—is effective if "preaching from the rooftops," as the Gospel says, is also accompanied by the example of a holy life. The noetic and dynamic aspects of the Faith and Revelation always go together. Preaching and holiness of life thus intersect, and from the one, the other can be recognized. Thus, "to speak" is to tell the truth and to live it, to put it into practice. When something injures one of these two dimensions, the cognitive and the volitional, or existential, or when it merely stands in the way, then one no longer has the strength to speak or, if one speaks, one does so without telling the truth. One becomes a poet by speaking through images and metaphors.[100]

It was a short step from "who am I to judge" to "who am I to speak." We are faced with the fact that the majority of bishops in this dramatic moment do not speak, do not intervene. This silence and inaction occur not only in the face of the practical denial of this or that truth of the Faith—such as the indissolubility of marriage, through the pastoral discernment of *Amoris Lætitia*, or the teaching on the sacrament of Holy Orders along with celibacy, which is one with it, inscribed in its sacramental ontology—but also in a more sensational way before the deplorable spectacle of the presence of pagan idols in the house of God during the Amazon Synod.

Certainly, the reasons one prefers not to speak, which today means especially not exposing oneself to the risk of severe punishment, are different. In fact, there are those who are afraid of losing their office. And there are those who are still convinced that they must strenuously defend above all else the unity of the Church and communion with the pope for the good of the faithful. They are forgetting that this unity and this communion with the Pontiff

---

[100] The Word of God makes known a truth (noetic aspect) and at the same time realizes what it means (dynamic aspect). God says and things are (see the creation account in Gen 1); Jesus reveals Himself, for example, as the Light of the world and heals the man born blind (Jn 9:1ff.). In this interweaving between the noetic and dynamic aspects of the Word of God, there is also the right link between doctrine and pastoral care.

are preserved by unity in the same faith professed by every single Catholic. One might think that, outwardly appearing to be in agreement with all that the Vatican or the pope himself says and does, the unity of the Church is manifested and the faithful are preserved from scandal. What could possibly be more scandalous to the faithful? Is there a more serious scandal than the loss of faith, or its use for its political ends, to the extent of being partisan, nurturing factions and resistance groups of all stripes and colors? There is much lamentation about the division between traditionalists and conservatives on the one hand, and progressives and pastoralists on the other. How can we reconcile them if the unity of the faith is lacking? The same discussion about the possibility of causing scandal to the faithful happened years ago, concerning the appropriateness, or not, of criticizing (in the etymological sense of distinguishing and judging) Vatican II, trying to study in depth the causes of the Church's decline in faith. Then it was deemed preferable to avoid touching on the subject of the last Council, above all to avoid troubling the faithful who are already being violently tossed to and fro by various doctrinal waves. In fact, this is a political rather than a theological argument. What makes someone think, in any case, that those who are the most lost are the laity rather than the clerics, who discuss the Faith according to their own ideas and often experiment with their ideologies at the expense of the laity? From a strange and novel conciliarism we have arrived at a novel papism. It is definitely not ultramontanism against Gallicanism, but rather a kind of papal absolutism, a blind submission to the head currently in charge, as if infallibility were ascribed to each and every word that is uttered and to each and every gesture.

However, the main reason why far too many of the faithful, clergy and laity alike, do not speak and do not even dare to show a sign of life seems to be that they no longer personally hold the Faith that they should proclaim and whose orthodoxy they should defend. This reluctance to speak manifested itself in regard to priestly celibacy, both with the event of the Amazon Synod and with the publication of Ratzinger and Sarah's explosive book on the subject. A mere handful came to the defense of celibacy. Many, nearly all, remained silent and waiting. For what? Why keep quiet? An answer was given by Cardinal Sarah in the book he coauthored. He too wonders why the bishops do not intervene in favor of celibacy, which is an apostolic tradition and which concerns them primarily, precisely as successors of the Apostles. For the fact is, they themselves are concerned by its binding nature. It is a doctrine which intimately concerns them. Yet though they live it faithfully, they do not feel like imposing it on the new generations. Sarah writes:

> Without this concrete experience, celibacy becomes a burden too heavy to carry. I get the impression that for some bishops from the West or even from South America, celibacy has become a heavy load. They remain faithful to it but no longer feel that they have the courage to impose it on future priests and on Christian communities because they themselves suffer from it. I understand them. Who could impose a burden on others without loving its deep meaning? Would that not be pharisaical? Nevertheless, I am certain that there is an error of perspective here. Although it is sometimes a trial, priestly celibacy, correctly understood, is liberating. It allows the priest to become established quite consistently in his identity as spouse of the Church.[101]

---

[101] Benedict XVI and Robert Cardinal Sarah, *From the Depths of Our Hearts: Priesthood, Celibacy and the Crisis of the Catholic Church* (San Francisco: Ignatius Press, 2020), 41 (e-pub).

Celibacy is no longer understood because the error of perspective indicates a doctrinal error and vice versa. As with celibacy, so too with marital indissolubility. It would have been very strange if, having opened a breach in the heart of indissoluble marriage during the two synods on the family, the indissolubility of the celibate priesthood according to the will of Christ and the Apostles had been respected. Marriage and celibacy either stand or fall together.[102] And precisely in order to preserve both, it is necessary to respect the fact that marriage and priesthood are mutually exclusive.

The problem is the silent apostasy in the Church, completely atypical because it is not the rejection of the Faith *sic et simpliciter*, a refusal to believe as such, but the transformation of the Faith into something else. We are faced with a liquid apostasy, which has its roots in the tried and tested attempt to separate the doctrinal aspect of Revelation from the pastoral one. This approach sees the beginning of preaching not in the truths to be believed, not in *what* to believe, but in *how* to believe, by judging its opportuneness and modalities. Here the *how* is analyzed by taking as a yardstick time in its mere chronological aspect of succession and constant flow. For such a view, this "flow" even becomes a theological place of God's Revelation. It is true that God communicates Himself to us in time, but He does so in a time that is an event of grace, the irruption of the mystery, a *kairos* that directs the *kronos*. Instead, modernist logic substitutes, for the qualitative time of God's visit, the mere quantitative flow. Given its ceaseless flow, it thus becomes superior to the "space"

---

[102] See, for extensive discussion of this point, Peter Kwasniewski, *Treasuring the Goods of Marriage in a Throwaway Society* (Manchester, NH: Sophia Institute Press, 2023).

of the encounter (to the mystery that reveals itself and remains present, *in primis* the incarnate Word) and to the revelatory event itself. The gap between the noetic and dynamic aspect of the Word of God, with the primacy of pastoral care over dogmatics, where an attempt is made to freeze the latter and to give space to praxeological activity, is now reflected in a gap in consciences, between intelligence and will. Thus the strength to speak is lost. Faith grows dim and dies.

For pastors to go back to speaking again, we must return to belief: the unity of faith must prevail in the Church over all other possible forms of unity. But for the whole Body of Christ, pastors and faithful, to return to belief, it is necessary to have a rule of faith, a norm that directs us, the *traditio fidei*. From a taboo word, *traditio* must once again become a theologically meaningful word, expressive of the Faith as a faithful *reception* and *transmission* through the Apostles of what Christ said and did, without personal additions and without subjective reductions. Only when the principle "I delivered to you as of first importance what I also received" (1 Cor 15:3) once again becomes the rule of preaching by bishops and priests, then and only then will the Faith once again be proclaimed, because it will also have come to be believed once again.

3

The Return of Nominalism

We live in a Church dominated by the words: "in my opinion."
The Amazon Synod held in Rome in October 2019, and more
broadly speaking the "synodal conversion" desired by Francis, have
become catalysts of dogmatic subjectivism.[103] Evidence of this can
be found in the final document of that Synod. After highlighting
the importance of a synodal conversion for the whole Church
according to the Amazonian fashion, it goes on to propose new
doctrines in contradiction to the doctrine of the Faith and its
consistent development. "To walk together the Church requires
a synodal conversion, synodality of the People of God under the
guidance of the Spirit in the Amazon," reads the final document
of the Amazon Synod (no. 86), according to the unofficial Italian
version offered by *L'Osservatore Romano*,[104] which conforms to

---

[103] One of the main minds behind the Amazon Synod, the Aus-
tro-Brazilian Bishop Erwin Kräutler, responding at the press
conference to the question about the possibility of the priestly
ordination of women, sets aside what the Church believes and
starts by saying "in my opinion." See the interview granted to
Edward Pentin: "Key Synod Father: Pan-Amazon Synod 'May
Be a Step to' Women Catholic Priests," *National Catholic Register*
online, October 9, 2019.

[104] October 28–29, 2019, p. 7.

the original Spanish.[105] The whole Church seemingly requires a synodal conversion in order to progress as one under the guidance of the Spirit in the Amazon. What is being said, with a slight play on words, is that the Church needs an Amazonian conversion. It must have an Amazonian face for a very practical reason, namely, to establish Amazonian ministries, as the three synodal documents systematically attest: the preparatory one (cf. nos. 12 and 14), the *Instrumentum Laboris* (nos. 107 and 116) and the final one (cf. nos. 86; 92 ff.). This is a conversion that cannot be fully achieved without first having invoked a "synodal conversion" as such, in order to encourage even a "conversion of the papacy" according to the request made in *Evangelii Gaudium* (no. 32).[106]

By virtue of an Amazonian conversion of the Church, the fruit of synodal conversion, we thus arrive at the Amazonian ministries, the real pastoral reason for which the Synod was called. By a sort

[105] "Para caminar juntos la Iglesia necesita una conversión Sinodal, sinodalidad del Pueblo de Dios bajo la guía del Espíritu en la Amazonía": www.sinodoamazonico.va/content/sinodoamazo-nico/es/documentos/documento-final-de-la-asamblea-especial-del-sinodo-de-los-obispo.html.

[106] This "synodal conversion" officially begins with the motu proprio *Episcopalis Communio* of September 15, 2018, in which the pope modified some norms governing the Synod, including those according to which, if the Pontiff expressly approves the final document, it partakes of the ordinary magisterium of the successor of Peter; if, instead, the Pontiff had conferred deliberative power on the Synod, the final document would participate in his ordinary magisterium as the successor of Peter, when ratified and promulgated by the latter. In that case the document is promulgated with the signature of the pope together with that of the other members. The final document of the Amazon Synod supports this vision and adopts the proclamation of an "integral conversion," including a synodal conversion.

of commutative principle implemented or to be implemented in the near future by this Synod, the new Amazonian ministries will become ecclesial ministries, signaling the shift toward the diaconal ordination of women (no. 103), whose hour has finally come. It will also shift toward the conferring of the priesthood on permanent deacons, even those who have a family, and thus no longer with the obligation of celibacy (no. 111). The Amazonian face will thus characterize the whole Church which presently seems to be guided by the "Spirit in the Amazon." In this way, however, alongside the nominalist use that is made of the Synod—with the Amazon Synod becoming a sort of ecumenical council, debating doctrines belonging to the deposit of faith—what is most disturbing is the clear intention to transform the Church by putting her into a state of permanent synodality, masking her one day with an Amazonian face, the next day, perhaps, with a German face (which bears a striking resemblance to that of the Amazon forest), and after that with any other sort of face that men might fancy to offer her. Yet this perennially synodal transformation, manifest in the swap of the doctrine of the faith for ministries and the synodal event, clearly shows a starting procedure heavily influenced by subjectivism. This is clearly to be seen in the expression "in my opinion," whose most remote source is to be sought specifically in cognitive Nominalism. Nominalism inevitably drifts into Pragmatism, and its final harbor is Materialism.

However, we need to keep in mind that we would never have arrived at this point if a larger and more significant event had not prevailed over the doctrinal content taught beforehand. I am speaking of the "Vatican II" event and the so-called "spirit of the Council" which prevailed in the texts of that great Synod itself. The fact that these texts, given their loquacious narrativity and ambivalence, lend themselves to accentuating their spirit over their doctrinal content must also be kept in mind when analyzing the context of the Amazon Synod, where the event prepares the ministries and the doctrine is enfolded in the event. This unity between event and word is united through a vocabulary in which words no longer express specific concepts, but are mostly, as John Locke (1632–1704) would have it, arbitrary assemblages of ideas, occasioned by the need to speak.[107]

This synodality, elevated to a new normative principle, seems obviously dissonant with the emphasis it places on the need to listen to the *sensus fidei*, extending participation to the faithful in addition to the bishops. In fact, however, what emerges from the recent synods is the proposal of doctrines that conflict with the *sensus fidei*. This is evident, for example, in the synodal attack on the family, through its attempt to open access to Communion for the divorced and remarried; in the synodal attack on young people, through its attempt to include the LGBT option among the various possibilities open to individuals (a failed attempt, due to a strong opposition on the part of the Catholic media); and finally in the Amazonian synodal attempt to alter the nature of the sacrament of Holy Orders as well as its associated celibacy. What *sensus fidei* are we talking about? Actually, this phrase *sensus fidei* has diverse meanings.

Nominalism, empiricism, and pragmatism

Nominalism is the path to trace if we wish to understand what is happening in the Church. There is certainly a nominalist tendency in the assertion "in my opinion," and in the subtle attempt to use terms of theological discourse in order to say something else. As

---

[107] See Paul J. Glenn, *The History of Philosophy* (London: B. Herder Book Co., 1948), 288.

we have said, though the word "synod" may now be employed, we can understand it as signifying "council." *"Sensus fidei"* is no longer what the Church believes *ubique, semper et ab omnibus*, but what a small group of people in power desires to affirm. Words no longer correspond to reality; they do not express reality for what it is. Nominalism is historically the high road that leads to Empiricism; it is also embraced by Positivism.

Let's consider its constitutive elements. According to the nominalist philosophical perspective, the idea to which universality was once attributed is, in reality, a mere collection of individual perceptions, a collective sensation, according to David Hume (1711–1776, in this indebted to Locke), "a term in habitual association with many other particular ideas."[108] An abstract concept does not differ essentially from sensation, of which it is only a transformation. Thus the Nominalism of Hume, John Stuart Mill (1806–1873), Herbert Spencer (1820–1903), Aldous Huxley (1894–1963) and Hippolyte Taine (1828–1893) is included in their Empiricism and Positivism. For Mill,

> Reality is sensation, therefore the concept is the synthesis of sense perception, deprived, through abstraction, of its specific elements. In brief, the concept is a word, the generality is a void. And, as reality is comprised of the senses, judgment is not the creator of reality, but the mere relationship between concepts, which founds the belief in objectivity—where objectivity means nothing more than mere consistency.[109]

---

[108] Maurice De Wulf, "Nominalism," in *The Catholic Encyclopedia* (New York: Robert Ampleton Company, 1911), 11:92.

[109] Guido De Ruggiero, *La filosofia contemporanea*, vol. II (Bari: Laterza, 1947), 18–19. Cf. De Wulf, "Nominalism," 93.

It is quite instructive to draw attention to the position of the Scottish empiricist David Hume on God's existence and the possibility of a natural religion. Since concepts do not express reality but are functions of thought, what they say is true and valid only if they can be verified by experience. In this way Hume, in his *Dialogues on Natural Religion*, calls into question the principle of causality, which Scholasticism had shown to be an effective means of arriving at the existence of God. In Hume's opinion, the order or compatibility between things and their finality (such as the compatibility between legs and walking) is not in itself proof that there is a designer who designs, except in the case in which experience shows us such an order. Could we ever come to understand from the growth of a single hair how a man begins to exist?[110] The main character of the *Dialogues on Natural Religion*, Philo, who actually is the voice of the author-philosopher himself, gives us an adequate picture of the essence of Empiricism, which rests on the foundation of Nominalism:

> This little agitation of the brain that we call "thought"—
> what special privilege does *it* have that entitles it to serve
> as the model of the entire universe? It looms large for *us*
> because *we* are always in presence of it; but sound philoso-
> phy ought carefully to guard against this kind of natural
> illusion.[111]

Thought, for Hume, is an illusion and only experience proves the truth of a thing or a relationship between cause and effect. However, we might address to Hume the following objection:

---

[110] See David Hume, *Dialogues on Natural Religion*, ed. Jonathan Bennett (2017), pp. 12–13, at www.earlymoderntexts.com/.

[111] Hume, 13.

in the event that a doctor fails to find the cause of the disease his patient is suffering from, could we say that that patient is not sick or that he will only truly be sick when the doctor himself has experienced the cause of his illness? And what if, in the meantime, the patient dies of that disease? This materializing of the principle of causality plays a significant role in Hume's denial of any possibility of natural religion, namely, of the capacity of human reason to know God. Hume does not want to declare himself an atheist or a miscreant. On the contrary, in his dialogues he repeatedly makes a profession of religiosity. The Scottish Empiricist does not know who God is. He only knows that He is far beyond the possibilities of his faculties. So it will be Philo who tells Cleanthes that a well-disposed mind's natural sentiment in this situation is to yearn for divine intervention:

> God will be content to remove or at least diminish this profound ignorance by giving mankind a particular revelation, *revealing* the nature, attributes, and operations of the divine object of our faith. A person, who has a correct understanding of the imperfection of natural reason, will willingly rush to embrace revealed truth, while the haughty dogmatist, persuaded that he can erect a perfect theological system with no other help than philosophy, will disdain all other help and reject this external support. To be skeptical from the philosophical point of view, in a man of letters, is the first and most essential step to becoming a solid Christian believer.[112]

Hume's skepticism paved the way for Immanuel Kant (1724–1804) who made God a *noumenon*, unknowable by the intellect,

---

[112] Hume, 62.

but accessible only by moral means. Thence, we arrive at the denial of God; He is said to be a mere projection of an idea originating in man. Representative in this respect is the position of Friedrich Nietzsche (1844–1900), according to whom the Christian need for redemption stems from a feeling of inadequacy. The feeling is caused by our being confronted with a perfect God, as well as by a longing to perform perfectly selfless actions. This need for redemption vanishes as soon as man eliminates the idea of God. In fact, Nietzsche is convinced that "if the idea of God is removed, so is also the feeling of 'sin' as a trespass against divine laws, as a stain in a creature vowed to God." The point we might make in response is that Christ is not a mere idea, but an incarnate person, and that redemption is an actual fact as well as a mystery. The premises, nonetheless, of the conclusion Nietzsche reached are nominalist.[113]

However, returning to Hume, the lesson he gives the "haughty dogmatist" is very interesting and topical: though we had once thought we could offer a complete theological system with the help of philosophy and metaphysics, this is something we must now renounce, since reason is incapable, and thought is an illusion that becomes reality only when this reality is sensorial, experiential.

In the words of Pope Francis, who seems to bring such reflections up to date, we could say that "realities are greater than ideas"[114] and that between the two, there is no correspondence. A strange sort of "humility" thus arises, characterizing the thought of many theologians who, aware of this, reject metaphysics as such and rely solely on fideism, that is, on the alethic justification

---

[113] Friedrich Nietzsche, *Human, All-Too-Human* (1878–80), trans. Helen Zimmern (London: T.N. Foulis, 1910), part 1, division 3, no. 133.

[114] Francis, Apostolic Exhortation *Evangelii Gaudium*, no. 233.

of dogma starting from faith alone. And they never leave the labyrinth of subjectivism. Fideism, in fact, is tied to subjectivism, as had happened with the Protestant Revolt. How often in our day do we hear that the doctrine of the faith is not to be viewed as stones to be thrown at those who do not believe, or at those who think differently from us, or that throwing truths and doctrinal formulas like stones is not Christian? This presupposes the kind of "humility" espoused by Hume, that of the intellect in an empiricist framework, and its foundation is the nominalist conception of thought.[115]

The ultimate result, and the reduction to absurdity of Empiricism, is Pragmatism. It sprang up in America in the context of business and business logic, but also developed in less affluent contexts. In fact,

> if reality is sensation and if the concept is merely the arbitrary abbreviation of sense experience, the value of the concept will be only that of an arbitrary fiction, but a convenient one. And on the other hand, if the concept is a purely subjective product, which does not reflect objective reality in itself, its validity can only be determined by success, by its success in that foreign reality. Hence the principle that ideas must be made to work in order to ensure their power, their practical efficiency.[116]

The simple agreement between individuals at the social level serves as the judge of what should be designated as truth, of

---

[115] See Pope Francis, *Without Jesus We Can Do Nothing: Being a Missionary in the World Today. A Conversation with Gianni Valente* (New London, CT: Twenty-Third Publications, 2020). See also *Amoris Lætitia*, no. 49.

[116] De Ruggiero, *La filosofia contemporanea*, 38–39.

what is true or false from a social and utilitarian point of view. A powerful pragmatism is also a hallmark of our day. Though the word "pastoral" is often employed, though we speak of "pastoral care" or of "pastoral projects," in fact this pastorality consists of a pragmatism that orients the theory, or better still it consists in a "praxeology"—a science of praxis from a theological point of view, derived from elevating pastorality to the supreme level of theology—that is in itself a theory of *praxis*. How can we qualify the work of the Amazon Synod if not as mere praxeology? The Amazonian missionary needs to justify the new Amazonian ministries, as we have said, and to justify the latter, moreover, as a new doctrine at odds with that received from Jesus through the Apostles.

The heterogeneity of words

In a scenario where Pragmatism prevails, that is, where thought is at the service of *praxis*, of the practical and more convenient resolution of the problems and challenges that time poses to faith, words frequently undergo sudden and multiple changes in meaning. Choosing a few examples from current theological jargon—in addition to the words "synod" and "*sensus fidei*" to which we have already referred—we can mention the words: "mercy," "mission," "pastoral," and finally "ecology." "Pastoral," one of the most nominalist expressions of the last sixty years, has now become "pastoral conversion," while "ecology" has now evolved into "ecological conversion" and "conversion to the territory."

Mercy is the fulfillment of justice according to the higher measure of love and forgiveness; it can never be granted without the presupposition of justice. Yet, for much of Francis's pontificate (broadly speaking from the outset, starting with the exaltation of Cardinal Kasper's book on the subject, up to the Jubilee of Mercy, which closed in November 2016), it seems that there has been a desire to emphasize God's forgiveness, but without any reference to truth or justice. This tendency goes as far as postulating the possibility for the divorced and remarried to receive Holy Communion, thanks to *Amoris Lætitia*; to the point of rehabilitating Luther, in a certain sense, through the Vatican celebrations for the five-hundredth anniversary of his revolt. This is characteristic of a forgiving justice which lacks, or even outright rejects, the idea of God's punitive justice. When "mercy" is proclaimed from the pulpit today, do the faithful still understand the meaning of the word?

The Church's mission is clearly expressed in Jesus's words to His Apostles before ascending to heaven: "Go therefore and make disciples of all nations, baptizing them in the name of the Father and of the Son and of the Holy Spirit, teaching them to observe all that I have commanded you" (Mt 28:19, 20). For Pope Francis, mission must never equal proselytism. However, it turns out to be a rather daunting task to avoid making proselytes or disciples through evangelization, and simultaneously to obey the words of the Lord. Mission is now properly expressed by employing a metaphor dear to the pope: "the outgoing Church." This means, in other words, abandoning the behavioral patterns of the past, abandoning the ready-made doctrinal recipes, letting go of one's own certainties of possessing the truth along with the desire to impose it on others, and so on and so forth. This occasions the Church's departure from her very self in order to become something other than herself, a more dynamic reality, which is finally fulfilled in the synodal process. Yet, at the same time, complicating the situation even further, the Holy Father expressed the wish for the month of October 2019 to be an Extraordinary Month of Mission, in order to celebrate the centenary of Benedict XV's encyclical, *Maximum Illud.* The latter, in fact, relaunched the mission of the Church not in view of initiating a process, with the perspective of an "outgoing Church," but according to the traditional imperative to go all over the world, to evangelize all men and convert them to Christ and His Gospel. Francis's missionary spirit risks becoming more strongly inward-looking because the purpose for which we must go out has been lost. So what has the Church's mission become in our day?

In this context, and alongside it, there is a sincere attempt to relaunch the missionary nature of the Church, passing from maintenance to mission. This attempt, however, even with the best of intentions, in reality leads to the same outcome as the one described above.[117] It begins with a purely factual observation: the Church is suffering from an identity crisis because, having become too introverted, it has renounced its missionary spirit. Being disciples of the Lord means being missionaries, making other disciples. True enough. But the point that needs to be made is precisely the contrary: if the Church's missionary spirit is in crisis, it is because the Church is experiencing an identity crisis. The effect must not be misconstrued as being the cause. However, the very essence of the Church is exchanged for missionary action when we are taught that the Church is essentially nothing other than its missionary activity, that being "apostolic" essentially means making other disciples. In reality, being apostolic means first and foremost that the Church, the Mystical Body of the Lord, is founded on the Apostles for the salvation of all peoples.

---

[117] In the English context, we can mention the very popular book by Fr. James Mallon, *Divine Renovation: Bringing Your Parish from Maintenance to Mission* (New London, CT: Twenty-Third Publications, 2014). I keep this book in mind in my following critique.

This mystery is to be brought to all men through evangelization, so that all peoples may become disciples of the Lord, members of His Body. Therefore, changing the Church's being, by substituting action for essence, even if with the laudable intention of reinvigorating its missionary spirit in an all-encompassing manner, is not a viable solution for remedying the standstill the mission has come to. It essentially means letting the Church's essence be absorbed into a continual becoming, a perpetual evolution. In the final analysis, it even means going out of the Church, which is indeed the very aim of "the outgoing Church." The mission is paralyzed because, for example, soteriology has been humanized and the Church has become merely "the people of God" embarking on a journey and picking up, along the way, all those who have been left by the wayside. The latter are invited to join, but they may just as well remain outside, supposing that suits them better, as they are already Christians without realizing it. So, why make disciples—proselytes, in the Scriptural sense (cf. Acts 2:10, 6:5, and 13:43)?

The word "pastoral" has become one of the most hackneyed expressions. Lacking a clear signification and a precise definition from the outset, ever since it was first proclaimed at the Second Vatican Council it has evolved over time and been used in a variety of ways. One of the main uses to which this word has been put has been to signal an anthropological shift in Christianity, in the name of *praxis*, which serves as a means both to embody and to assess theology as such. If theology is nothing more than pastoral, in the sense that pastoral care becomes the gauge of the historical compatibility of a doctrine over time, then theology is no longer itself. Pastoral care, also synonymous with the missionary spirit, is not only the end, but becomes, in this anthropocentric context, the means as well. Thus, we arrive at "pastoral conversion," which requires the Church to go out of herself, a Church now understood in her pastoral state of becoming. This understanding calls into question the papacy itself and the central structures of the Church.[118] Thus it seems that pastoral care converts the hierarchical Church into an increasingly insubstantial reality, with less centralized power, and closer to the existential peripheries.

Finally, with the encyclical *Laudato Si'* (May 24, 2015), and with its successor document, the apostolic exhortation *Laudate Deum* (October 4, 2023), we have entered a new phase of the pontificate of Pope Francis. The key word has ceased to be "mercy"— since the end of the Jubilee dedicated to it, this word has hardly been uttered—and we have moved on to a new buzzword: "ecology." Ecology in this case signifies the care of the common home, of the Earth or "Mother Earth." Previous popes had always linked the ecological duty of respect for creation to an integral ecology of the human person in relation to God. Now, the human person is viewed in relation to ecology, which is the commitment to avoid exploiting the earth. The Earth has also become a particular geographical territory and a source of revelation, as in the case of the Amazon region, according to the dictates of the *Instrumentum Laboris*, which served as a guide to the synodal proceedings. An "ecological conversion" will thus be achieved, which involves (as per the *Instrumentum Laboris* no. 104) "recovering the myths and updating the rites and community celebrations that contribute significantly to the process of ecological conversion." Henceforth, ecology and ecological conversion go far beyond their original meaning and lead to an understanding of ecology as a natural (or pantheistic?) bond between man and nature, to be celebrated in myth and to be reflected in community celebrations. The synodal

---

[118] See Francis, Apostolic Exhortation *Evangelii Gaudium*, no. 32.

majority also decided to create an Amazonian rite. So, what exactly is "ecology"?

Each key word of this theological newspeak receives as many meanings as those attributed to it by the knowing subject. It is easy to understand why this leads to a dead end for any real communication; not only is there no longer any theology that expresses the content of the Faith (as if that were still important!), there is not even any comprehensible content. Is this the reason why Vatican communication is increasingly going haywire?

Heterogeneity of ends

The heterogeneity of words necessarily leads to a kind of heterogeneity of ends. A new doctrine, though employing the same words, now lends itself to achieving ends different from those pursued up until a few years ago by the magisterium of the Church. If words no longer express reality, whose essence they seek to express, then they easily become an instrument of power, the vehicle of a will to power. At times they are demagogic, at times opportunistic, but most often revolutionary in aim. Words become mere instruments to achieve an end, which is not the knowledge of truth but the propagation of one's own ideas. If this way of doing things prevails, and ends up affirming the opinions of the majority, then the doctrine of the Faith, subject to the winds of every fashion, will be torn to shreds. It is unavoidable, however, even for the most intransigent nominalist worldview, that a doctrine (an idea) expresses reality: it will express it insofar as it is convenient, useful for the present. Nominalism is fulfilled and confirmed in Pragmatism.

A way out of this linguistic impasse, which no longer allows us to know the Faith for what it is or to judge a theology or a pastoral vision for what it represents, is obviously at hand: it consists in a return to scholastic realism. Metaphysics and logic must be studied in seminaries. Universals do not deceive us, because they derive from reality. They express reality as what it truly is and are not mere intellectual fantasies or rather sophisticated sensations. Concepts are derived from reality and therefore correspond to real things, to what is; concepts are that by which our intellect masters the multiplicity of experience with a penetration into essences. The dogmas of the faith that we profess are not empty formulas, but express the truth that Christ taught us and that the Church has transmitted to us uninterruptedly. If we say "mission" or "conversion" we can only mean what Christ told us and what the Church has continually taught and transmitted. The word "mission" (to take just one example, which can summarize this topic) is derived from the teaching of Christ and the Apostles and is not a hollow word, an empty vessel which anyone can fill according to the fashions of the times. If we change its meaning because we do not know what it is, and instead learn what it is from the human sciences or from human religions, it is as if we would change reality and change the Gospel. The intellect does not deceive us, because reality is fundamentally not a fiction and cannot be fictitious. Christ is no mere fiction. We urgently need to reclaim a theological vocabulary.

4

"The Outgoing Church" or Going Out of the Church?

Let us now examine critically a key concept of Pope Francis's teaching: "the outgoing Church." This concept connects a reality with a metaphor. The reality is the Church, the mystery of faith revealed by God in Christ and constituted hierarchically upon the Apostles and their successors; the metaphor which aims to explain this reality in a novel way is "outgoing," "going forth," with an allusion to Israel's exodus from Egypt. The fact that a figure is used to explain the reality and not the other way around complicates the expression and therefore makes it difficult to understand unambiguously. Hence the main difficulty is in the attempt to clarify what is implied by this "going forth" and how we ought to understand the mission of the Church that goes forth. I present my analysis in three parts. We will firstly see what, according to Pope Francis, is meant by "outgoing Church." Next, how the pairing of these two terms substantially alters the Church's mission. Third, what the possible hermeneutical repercussions of this might be, since they open the door to interpretative conflict.

The outgoing Church: What is it?

Francis began to speak systematically of the "outgoing Church" in the programmatic document of his pontificate, *Evangelii Gaudium* (abbreviation *EG*, nn. 20–24), though as yet in rather general terms. A definition of the "Church that goes forth" can be found in no. 24 of this document:

> The Church which "goes forth" is a community of missionary disciples who take the first step, who are involved and supportive, who bear fruit and rejoice. An evangelizing community knows that the Lord has taken the initiative, he has loved us first (cf. 1 Jn 4:19), and therefore we can move forward, boldly take the initiative, go out to others, seek those who have fallen away, stand at the crossroads and welcome the outcast.

In no. 49 of *EG*, on the other hand, the pope makes a very strong appeal, by associating this "going forth" with the abandoning of one's own security, with being a wounded and even dirty Church:

> Let us go forth, then, let us go forth to offer everyone the life of Jesus Christ. Here I repeat for the entire Church what I have often said to the priests and laity of Buenos Aires: I prefer a Church which is bruised, hurting and dirty because it has been out on the streets, rather than a Church which is unhealthy from being confined and from clinging to its own security. I do not want a Church concerned with being at the center and which then ends by being caught up in a web of obsessions and procedures. If something should rightly disturb us and trouble our consciences, it is the fact that so many of our brothers and sisters are living without the strength, light and consolation born of friendship with Jesus Christ, without a community of faith to support them, without meaning and a goal in life.

These considerations, however, prompt us to reflect on the historical moment in which we are living. The Church, as never before, finds herself engulfed in a moral crisis of terrifying proportions. Drawing a logical inference from these words, should we think that Francis prefers a dirty and deplorable Church like the present one, immersed in a sex-abuse crisis, rather than a Church that draws from doctrinal and moral clarity the strength to serve others in truth and honesty? Benedict XVI's notes, written in view of the Vatican summit on abuse, held from February 21 to 24, 2019,[119] probed deeply into this issue. For the first time, setting aside a generic clericalism, the true root of the problem was grasped: the theological-moral collapse into which the Church is plunged, due to its many exponents having embraced the revolutionary ideas of the 1960s. Pope Francis at present seems unwilling to discuss the causes of sexual abuse in the Church, including the vices of impurity and homosexuality, which have been justified through a subjectivist theological-moral vision. This has led to a practical relativism.

Doctrinal references to the "Church that goes forth" can be found in some more original teachings. One of the most important is the first General Audience of Francis on Wednesday, March 27, 2013, in which the pope said that living Holy Week means entering ever more deeply into the logic of God:

> It means entering into the logic of the Gospel. Following and accompanying Christ, staying with him, demands "coming out of ourselves," requires us to be outgoing; to

---

[119] The full text of "The Church and the Scandal of Sexual Abuse" may be found at the Catholic News Agency (*inter alia*), www. catholicnewsagency.com/news/41013/full-text-of-benedict-xvi-essay-the-church-and-the-scandal-of-sexual-abuse.

come out of ourselves, out of a dreary way of living faith that has become a habit, out of the temptation to withdraw into our own plans which end by shutting out God's creative action. God came out of himself to come among us, he pitched his tent among us to bring to us his mercy that saves and gives hope. Nor must we be satisfied with staying in the pen of the ninety-nine sheep if we want to follow him and to remain with him; we too must "go out" with him to seek the lost sheep, the one that has strayed the furthest. Be sure to remember: coming out of ourselves, just as Jesus, just as God came out of himself in Jesus and Jesus came out of himself for all of us.[120]

The "Church that goes forth" is here linked to God's "coming out of himself" to come among us. However, this expression requires clarification since it gives rise to erroneous interpretations. God is and remains Himself even when He becomes man. Therefore the Son, God from God, in His incarnation did not come out of Himself. He remained in Himself, in His divine nature, taking from the womb of the Virgin Mary His human nature and uniting it to the divine nature in the one person of the Logos. The Son did indeed come forth from the bosom of the Father to become man, yet while forever remaining in His bosom, *in sinu Patris* (cf. Jn 1:18). Even now as man He remains forever facing the Father, because He and the Father are one (Jn 10:30). A God who would "come out of himself" might suggest that God, by becoming man, surpasses Himself; this could be understood in an idealistic-Hegelian sense, in which the negative, the idea beyond itself, but also sin or, in this case, human nature, are necessary for

---

[120] In *L'Osservatore Romano*, March 28, 2013, p. 8.

the Spirit (God) to become fully Himself by embracing what is outside of Himself, in a greater synthesis. This would be in fact a unity of the positive and the negative, of God and man, of the sacred and the profane, of good and evil. Nothing would escape a divine synthesis that encompasses everything, surpasses everything, and justifies everything in an endless dialectical process.

In one of the first interviews given to Fr. Antonio Spadaro, on August 19, 2013, Francis applied this concept of "God coming out of himself" to the Church, saying:

> Instead of being just a Church that welcomes and receives by keeping the doors open, let us try also to be a church that finds new roads, that is able to step outside itself and go to those who do not attend Mass, to those who have quit or are indifferent. The ones who quit sometimes do it for reasons that, if properly understood and assessed, can lead to a return. But that takes audacity and courage.[121]

The need for the Church to step outside itself was reiterated by Pope Francis in *EG* when he warns about the risk—one of the gravest—of "spiritual worldliness," by which he means the reduction of spirituality to a thing of appearances and ambitions, and thus disconnected from the Gospel call to serve. This is a danger that can be avoided by "making the Church constantly go out from herself, keeping her mission focused on Jesus Christ, and her commitment to the poor" (no. 97). It is all a matter of "stepping out of oneself," which refers especially to the need always to reach out to others, to our brethren and to all men in need of salvation, by avoiding an exclusively inward focus on ourselves. However, if one reflects in a metaphysical mode on this appeal,

---

[121] Reported in *L'Osservatore Romano*, September 21, 2013, p. 6.

which is a key concept of Pope Francis's teaching, it seems that it cannot be anything but difficult for the faithful to grasp and comprehend. Even if the Church—in her members and not in herself—wished to go out of herself, from the sacristies and from her own paralyzing convictions, to go toward others, she could never *go out of herself*, in the sense of abandoning her mystery. If she did so, she would no longer be herself, she would be transformed into something else, she would become a mere *societas humana* made by us. The only possible way to go forth is "to go into all the world," leaving the physical place of the Upper Room, but never leaving the Church as she is, but, on the contrary, building her up in every place where the Gospel is proclaimed. This "going out from herself" on the part of the Church seems to take for granted a multifaceted, or at least a twofold, meaning which the interpreter on duty can give you, even if it seems obvious that the metaphysical meaning is being privileged (as will become evident). By now, we can affirm that it is the ontological meaning of "going out" that prevails (even if the aim is not strictly speaking metaphysical): the "Church that goes forth" has gone out of the Church, in the sense of being affected in her very being and not simply in her way of presenting herself to the world. This is a "going forth" that privileges a new day and age and, precisely for this reason, necessarily affects the mystery-Church, which it tries to reshape. It means going out as a movement, a process of transformation of the Church into a body of doctrine which is more pastoral or more missionary, less rigid, open to all needs and understood primarily in a social way.

Moreover, going out of the Church *as such* principally means leaving the Church that has existed up to now, until the Second Vatican Council—becoming a new, more vibrant community, embarking on a journey. This presupposes conceiving of the Church exclusively as the "people of God," contrary to, or in any case without, the concept of the "mystical body" of Christ.[122] In fact, speaking to the Jesuits of the Baltic countries on September 23, 2018, Pope Francis said precisely this: what must be done today is to ensure that "the Council makes its way into the Church." There will be "a profound spiritual renewal of the Church" when we come to recognize, with *Lumen Gentium* 12, that she is the people of God, in opposition to the "perversion of the Church today," which is clericalism.[123] This profound change will come, therefore, when all unanimously recognize that the Church is the People of God. Would the Church understood as "body of Christ" be guilty of encouraging clericalism due to its hierarchical nature?

This initial teaching on God's coming out of Himself and thus of the Church coming out of herself was later reiterated by the

---

[122] During the course of 2014, Pope Francis dedicated a series of catecheses to the mystery of the Church. Among these, one concerns the Church as the Body of Christ (October 22, 2014). The theme, however, is missing in his programmatic documents, in particular in *EG*, in which instead the connotation of the Church as People of God is very recurrent.

[123] "'I believe the Lord wants a change in the Church': A private dialogue with the Jesuits in the Baltics," in *La Civiltà Cattolica* (2018), IV, 105–13; online at www.laciviltacattolica.com/i-believe-the-lord-wants-a-change-in-the-church-a-private-dialogue-with-the-jesuits-in-the-baltics/. See also Walter Insero, *Il popolo secondo Francesco: Una rilettura ecclesiologica* (Vatican City: Libreria Editrice Vaticana, 2018). In his address at the end of the Meeting on the Protection of Minors in the Church (February 24, 2019), the pope remarked on the antithesis between People of God and clericalism: "It will be precisely this holy People of God who will liberate us from the plague of clericalism, which is the fertile ground for all these abominations," in *L'Osservatore Romano*, February 25–26, 2019, p. 11.

pope. Welcoming the participants in the General Assembly of the Focolare Movement, on September 26, 2014, Francis referred to his first General Audience, in which he had presented the Christological motif of the outbound Church, and also added another detail concerning the outbound evangelization Christians must engage in. Then there was mention of outbound dialogue, thanks to Hebrews 13:13 and the image of the Church as "field hospital," in which accurate diagnoses are avoided (that is, philosophical and theological "Byzantinisms"), but where doctors are content with bandaging the bleeding wounds with all the makeshift equipment that chance might offer. The Pontiff said:

> To do this, it is necessary to become an expert in that art of "dialogue," and that doesn't come cheap. We cannot be satisfied with half measures, we must not tarry, but rather, with God's help, aim high and broaden our perspective! And to do this we must go forth boldly "to him outside the camp, bearing abuse for him" (Heb 13:13). He awaits us in the trials and the cries of our brethren, in the wounds of society and in the interrogations of the culture of our time. It pains the heart when, in front of a church, a humanity with so many wounds, moral wounds, existential wounds, wounds caused by war, which we feel every day, we see how Christians begin to engage in philosophical, theological, spiritual "byzantinisms," whereas what we need is an outgoing spirituality. Go forth with this spirituality: do not remain securely locked inside. This is no good. This is "Byzantinism"! Today we have no right to this sort of Byzantinesque reflection. We must go forth! Because—as I have said on other occasions—the Church is like a field hospital. And when you go to a field hospital, the first task

is to treat people's wounds, not to measure their choles-
terol... That will come later... Is that clear?[124]

In this speech, the theme of the "outgoing Church" is justified
with the help of a quotation from the Letter to the Hebrews. Let
us briefly analyze the context of the biblical phrase quoted (Heb
13:11–13), where, in short, Paul expounds "our worship by presenting it as a direct consequence of Christ's expiatory death."[125]
Here the text invites us to go forth "outside the camp" or "outside
the enclosure" in reference to the Feast of the Jewish Atonement
and therefore to the Redemption of Christ (cf. Heb 9:7–9; 4:14;
9:24; 10:20; Lev 16:27). In fact, as the bodies of the sacrificed
animals were burned outside the encampment and only their blood
was brought by the high priest into the sanctuary, so also Jesus,
to sanctify His people, died outside the walls of the Holy City
and His blood was brought by Him into the sanctuary of heaven.

The fundamental question (taking into account this Christian
sacrificial context that surpasses and fulfills that of the Old Testament) concerns the precise meaning of that "let us go forth to
him outside the camp, bearing abuse for him" (Heb 13:13). Most
commentators seem inclined to recognize in it a metaphorical
meaning of going out of Judaism, that is, of a still material cult
propagated by Jewish ritual practices, which can lead to deviation
from the Faith. On the contrary, by accepting the dishonor of
Christ, His Cross, "a stumbling block to Jews and folly to Gentiles" (cf. 1 Cor 1:23), we are led into true worship and the true
sanctuary. The people to whom the epistle was addressed were
Christians coming from Judaism whom the sacred author asks

---

124 In *L'Osservatore Romano*, September 27, 2014, p. 7.
125 Nello Casalini, *Agli Ebrei: Discorso di esortazione* (Jerusalem:
Franciscan Printing Press, 1992), 437.

to leave their comfortable position as Jews tolerated by the Roman Empire and to be ready instead to suffer dishonor through their following of Christ.[126] To this interpretation can be added the other, more literal signification, which sees in the exhortation to go "outside the enclosure" (*exo tes paremboles*) an invitation to do what Christ did in His offering of Himself for us; by adding "to him," the author transforms this going forth into an image in order to invite us to adhere to Christ in faith with our whole life.[127] This more theological and spiritual interpretation seems to be preferred for two reasons:[128] firstly, because in 13:9 the author exhorts us not to be carried away by "diverse and strange teachings." If the reader were a Jew, he could not be told that his doctrine is strange, that is, foreign. Secondly, because in 13:10 a clear distinction is made between "us" and "those who serve the tent," that is, those who adhere to Judaism. So it seems that neither the author nor his readers adhere to it. Therefore, they should not go out of that to which they do not belong; they should go instead to Christ by adhering to Him sincerely. The "camp" or "enclosure" from which one must go forth has an important spiritual meaning. Among other things, it alludes to leaving the world to head toward Christ, as St. John Chrysostom teaches in a homily on Hebrews, when he says that we must imitate our Savior, who chose to go to the Cross for our salvation; we must abandon the world and its empty concerns.[129]

---

[126] See, e.g., F.F. Bruce, *The Epistle to the Hebrews* (Grand Rapids, MI: Eerdmans, 1964), 381; The Navarre Bible, *The Letter to the Hebrews* (Dublin: Four Courts Press, 2003), 145.

[127] See Herbert Braun, *An die Hebräer* (Tübingen: Mohr, 1984), 467.

[128] This is what is maintained by Casalini, *Agli Ebrei*, 437.

[129] St. John Chrysostom, *Homily on the Letter to the Hebrews*, 33, cited in Navarre Bible *Hebrews*, 145.

At any rate, according to the Letter to the Hebrews, which envisions Christ as the center of our worship and our adherence to faith, this going forth has a very elevated theological and spiritual value. Christian life is indeed an "exodus," but in which we go toward Christ in the truth of the doctrine of the faith, transforming our very existence into a "sacrifice of praise to God, that is, the fruit of lips that acknowledge his name," as the next verse adds (Heb 13:14). The Christian exodus—"here we have no lasting city, but we seek the city which is to come" (Heb 13:14)—is here understood in relation to the Old Testament ritual exodus with the celebration of the Passover, the covenant of Sinai and the Day of Atonement, finding their fulfillment in the Passion, Death, and Resurrection of Christ.[130] Our sacrifice, therefore, cannot but perfectly express Christian life, which becomes a ritual life of adoration of God in view of the definitive vision in heaven. Nothing, therefore, suggests that the Hebrews in this pericope are being told to distance themselves from the doctrinal, moral, and cultic aspects of Christian life or of the Church as they have experienced them up to now. On the contrary, putting together the exegetic-theological data of our pericope, we can conclude that it exhorts us to embrace the true exodus, which is to adhere to Christ with the Church—that is, with a true faith that becomes a liturgy of praise and, consequently, true life.

The mission of the "outgoing Church"

According to Francis, this outgoing, this going forth is about having a missionary spirit and evangelizing, but—first and foremost— being pastoral, so as to avoid fixating on the rigor of doctrine (useless byzantinism), and going outside the camp in order not to

---

[130] See Navarre Bible *Hebrews*, 145–46.

miss an opportunity to bind up the wounds, to console. "Pastoral conversion" (*EG* 27) plays a prominent role here. Interposing itself between mission as norm and effective evangelization through the Christian proclamation addressed to all, this pastoral conversion seems from time to time to determine the fate of the mission itself. Mission is the going forth from the Church, from what she herself is, to go to the peripheries, to the poor, to the disinherited, but does not necessarily and unequivocally imply preaching Christ and leading the Gentiles to Christ in His Church. It is necessary to decipher correctly what "pastoral conversion" is, even if this is not always easy, given the fluidity of the concept of pastorality that has predominated since the Second Vatican Council.[131] What we clearly know is that it is necessary to "devote the necessary effort to advancing along the path of a pastoral and missionary conversion which cannot leave things as they presently are" (*EG* 25). Going forth becomes pastoral conversion and pastoral conversion means change.

"Going forth" is becoming increasingly important, even if this involves going forth from the faith of the Church in its dogmatic formulation. According to Pope Francis, the pastoral care of vocations requires a Church that is on the move. Speaking at the Conference on Pastoral Work for Vocations, sponsored by the Congregation for the Clergy, on October 21, 2016, he said:

> We have to learn to *go out from* our rigidness that makes us incapable of communicating the joy of the Gospel, out from the standardized formulas that often prove to be

---

[131] See Serafino M. Lanzetta, "Il carattere 'pastorale' del Vaticano II tra interpretazioni coerenti (cioè logiche) e interpretazioni incoerenti (cioè arbitrarie)," in *Divinitas Verbi: Quaderni di epistemologia teologica (Teologia e Magistero oggi),* 1 (2017): 27–58.

anachronistic, out from the preconceived analyses that classify the lives of people into cold categories. Go out from all of this.[132]

What is bewildering, however, is the fact that, on the one hand, though there is a vibrant exhortation on the part of the Pontiff to go forth as missionaries of the Church,[133] on the other hand, by insisting on the need to go forth rather than on the duty to lead all Gentiles to Christ, there is a risk not only of this going forth becoming a slogan which conveys other ideas, but particularly of the Church's mission being halted and of the Church itself turning its focus ever more inward, finding itself crushed under its own weight. There is, in fact, in Francis's exhortations, an encouragement to be missionary, as reiterated by the Second Vatican Council and in line with the previous magisterium, but also a serious reprimand and a warning against proselytism.[134] The Second Vatican Council's decree on missions teaches us that the Lord Jesus, to whom the Father gave "all authority in heaven and on earth" (Mt 28:18), before ascending to heaven, founded His Church as the sacrament of salvation and sent His Apostles into the whole world, as He Himself had been sent by the Father. Jesus commanded His followers: "Go therefore and make disciples of all nations, baptizing them in the name of the Father and of the Son and of the Holy Spirit, teaching them to observe all that I have commanded you" (Mt 28:19–20) and also: "Go into all the world and preach the Gospel to the whole creation. He who believes

---

[132] In *AAS* 11 (2016): 1215.

[133] See, e.g., *EG*, nos. 19–49.

[134] See, among many references, the Morning Meditation in the Domus Sanctæ Marthæ Chapel, September 9, 2016, in *L'Osservatore Romano*, September 10, 2016.

and is baptized will be saved; but he who does not believe will be condemned" (Mk 16:15). We read in *Ad Gentes* no. 5:

> Whence the duty that lies on the Church of spreading the faith and the salvation of Christ, not only in virtue of the express command which was inherited from the Apostles by the order of bishops, assisted by the priests, together with the successor of Peter and supreme shepherd of the Church, but also in virtue of that life which flows from Christ into His members. . . .

Thus, there is apparently quite a daunting task to harmonize Christ's command to make disciples of all nations with the warning against making proselytes. If proselytism meant coercion of the will of others, then the error would be obvious. The crisis of eschatology—a crisis seen in the inability or unwillingness to speak of the Four Last Things and the failure to recognize that eternity is not only a condition but also a metaphysical place—along with the lack of a clear definition of what "salvation" means, has also impacted the concept of "mission," separating it from its goal, which is the salvation of all Gentiles in Christ, in and by means of His Mystical Body, for the sake of attaining eternal life. A mission without a clear eschatological objective easily becomes mere moral paraenesis, along with a large dose of purely social concerns. If the boundary between the sacred and the profane is blurred, there will no longer be any difference between the specific mission *ad gentes*, the new evangelization, the care of souls (tasks eminently missionary according to a hierarchical-missionary priority, although their boundaries are not clearly definable)[135] and the Church's social commitment; a mission which is nonetheless

---

[135] See John Paul II, Encyclical *Redemptoris Missio*, no. 34.

for the sake of building the heavenly City. Without further distinctions, "mission" can easily be interchanged with welcoming refugees and the poor, openness, listening—but it will no longer have a univocal meaning with regard to the Church's specific mission (making disciples of all nations) and an analogous sense for the new evangelization and the care of souls.

An image and a process

What is characteristic of Pope Francis's manner of speaking is the use of image and metaphor. The image, at times metaphorical, which is of concern to us in this case is "outgoing," "going forth," which is used to describe the mission of the Church. Sometimes it seems that the pope takes poetic license to say things that not everyone else can permit themselves to say. But metaphorical speech does not facilitate the understanding of the mystery-Church, which thus becomes blurred, with indiscernible contours. There is a risk of losing sight of the Church's visible aspect, the incarnate one, and of referring only to its invisible aspect. Mission, according to this new understanding, as we have said, does not always or simply mean the Church's mission as enunciated by the Gospel and outlined by the Catechism. Instead, it means a distancing from the Church for another sort of missionary purpose, namely the Church's renewal according to the pastoral exigencies dictated by the historical moment in which the Church happens to find itself—a moment that could well be called "postconciliar." The life of the mission, however, in this case is detached from the essence of the Church. This is because it seems that movement precedes being, and action is placed before essence, before *being* in and of itself.

The Church that goes forth, as we have said, presupposes almost exclusively the concept of the Church as People of God, from *Lumen Gentium* (11–12). If the Church is not first of all a mystery and therefore the Body of Christ, but merely a people, the ecclesial structure can easily degenerate into a simple program of action. Instead, as Joseph Ratzinger explains, the Church can be the people of God *in* and *by means of* the body of Christ. The people called to become Church form the Body of Christ, with a clear Eucharistic connotation (cf., e.g., 1 Cor 10:17). Thus, the Church is the People of God through communion with Christ in the Holy Spirit.[136] Then again, the expression "people of God" in the New Testament designates almost exclusively the people of Israel and not the Church, which is called *ekklesia*. Yet, in the years following the Council, especially through liberation theology, the focus was exclusively on this aspect of the Church as People of God. This soon became detached from God and became the sovereignty of the people against the ruling classes. A people rose up against the hierarchical structure of the Church. An interesting analysis of this postconciliar euphoria, which adopted certain doctrinal categories and elevated them to political absolutes, is found in a conference given in 2000 by Cardinal Ratzinger, then Prefect of the Congregation for the Doctrine of the Faith.[137] The latter pointed out, in his speech, with the Bochum exegete Werner Berg, that "people of God" is a rather rare biblical concept that expresses the "kinship" with God; it is therefore to be understood

---

[136] See Joseph Ratzinger, *Popolo e Casa di Dio in S. Agostino* (Milan: Jaca Book, 1978); original German edition: *Volk und Haus Gottes in Augustins Lehre von der Kirche* (Munich: Zink, 1954). See also Fr. Blanco Sarto, "Mysterium, communio et Sacramentum. La Ecclesiologia eucaristica di Joseph Ratzinger," in *Annales Theologici* 25 (2011): 241–70.

[137] Joseph Ratzinger, "L'ecclesiologia della Costituzione *Lumen Gentium*," in Rino Fisichella, ed., *Il Concilio Vaticano II: Recezione e attualità alla luce del Giubileo* (San Paolo: Cinisello Balsamo, 2000), 66–82.

according to a supernatural meaning, in relation to God, and never lends itself to being interpreted as a cry of protest against ministers. Precisely this definition of Church was at the center of the postconciliar effervescence, where the term "people" was adopted but bereft of its genitive "God." Thus, the Church herself became superfluous. Among other things, Ratzinger said:

> The crisis of the Church as it is reflected in the concept of People of God, is a "crisis of God"; it is the consequence of abandoning the essential. What remains is merely a struggle for power. There is enough of this elsewhere in the world, there is no need of the Church for this.[138]

Liberation theology relied, from the exegetical point of view, precisely on this notion of "people of God"—a people that is constituted above all in the exodus from Egyptian slavery to the promised homeland, interpreting in a more symbolic rather than literal way Israel's passage through the Red Sea and its pilgrimage in the desert (whose historicity it strongly called into question). In a miscellany on the occasion of the sixtieth anniversary of Gustavo Gutiérrez, one of the founding fathers of liberation theology, Norman Gottwald offers an interesting analysis of the Exodus as an event and a process.[139] Extolling Gutiérrez's groundbreaking book *Liberation Theology*, Gottwald sees as his main merit the fact that he highlighted the biblical exodus as a cornerstone in order to eliminate and transcend the

---

[138] Ibid., 68–69.

[139] Norman K. Gottwald, "The Exodus as Event and Process: A Test Case in the Biblical Grounding of Liberation Theology," in *The Future of Liberation Theology: Essays in Honor of Gustavo Gutiérrez*, ed. M.H. Ellis and O. Maduro (Maryknoll, NY: Orbis Books, 1989), 250–60.

old model with its "distinction of planes." The old model left Christianity divided between "the profane" (worldly concerns) and "the sacred" (otherworldly concerns). In Gottwald's opinion, it is specifically Gutiérrez who depicts in an exemplary way this state of exodus of theology, now intermingled with sociology and politics, when he says:

> The liberation of Israel is a political action. It is breaking away from a situation of despoliation and misery and the beginning of the construction of a just and comradely society. . . . The Exodus is the long march towards the promised land in which Israel can establish a society free from misery and alienation. Throughout the whole process, the religious event is not set apart. It is placed in the context of the entire narrative, or more precisely, it is its deepest meaning.[140]

Moreover, the Exodus seen as a process, Gottwald writes, is

> the movement of a people from a situation of slavery to a situation of liberty, from a collective life determined by others to a collective life that is self-determining and this movement is conceived as an adventure in the face of risk and uncertainty, as consequences of a "break for freedom." This entails the possibility and, in appropriate circumstances, the actual accomplishing of a social and political revolution.[141]

---

[140] Gustavo Gutiérrez, *A Theology of Liberation: History, Politics, and Salvation* (Maryknoll, NY: Orbis Books, 1988), 88–89; original Spanish edition: *Teología de la liberación: Perspectivas* (Lima: CEP, 1971).

[141] Gottwald, "Exodus," 253.

"The Outgoing Church" or Going Out of the Church?

This is the very essence of liberation theology. The central point, however, is the unity between the sacred and the profane, which are no longer juxtaposed to one another, but one within the other: the sacred is to be found in the profane, where, however, the profane becomes sacred and sacredness is stripped of its sumptuous garments and meddles with the messy affairs of everyday life. Behind this unity and overcoming of the barrier between sacred and profane, between sacred history and profane history, lies Karl Rahner.[142]

If the word "people" were replaced by "Church" and the word "exodus" by "outgoing" (not only as an event but above all as a process) is there not the risk of arriving at the same conclusions? Pope Francis wants processes to occur because time is greater than space (see *EG 222–25*). We must not occupy a space, by remaining rigid and motionless, but move, by initiating a process, a change. Processes build a people (cf. *EG 224*). What will be the culmination of this process? When will the Church truly and completely step out of herself? Prioritizing time obviously does not even allow such questions to be asked.

Finally, in this process of change, pastoral care plays a primary role: it converts the mission from being doctrinal to becoming an outgoing movement for a reform of the Church and her

---

[142] See Karl Rahner, *Foundations of Christian Faith: An Introduction to the Idea of Christianity*, trans. William V. Dych (New York: Crossroad, 2016; first trans. 1978), 116ff.; original German: *Grundkurs des Glaubens: Einführung in den Begriff des Christentums* (Freiburg im Breisgau: Herder, 1976). The grace of divine self-communication—supposedly God's revelation in history—encompasses and pervades the profane world and man as such, making man open to grace insofar as he is open to the infinite horizon of knowledge (which is held to be God, and so one falls into ontologism).

administrative apparatus.[143] Indeed, "the papacy and the central structures of the universal Church also need to hear the call to pastoral conversion" (*EG* 32). As recently revealed thanks to a leak by some journalists and to the harsh criticism expressed by Cardinal Müller,[144] and confirmed by the motu proprio *Praedicate Evangelium* of March 19, 2022, the reform of the Roman Curia has been intensely impacted by this "pastoral conversion," to the point that a super-dicastery of Evangelization stands at the head of all the others. The Congregation for the Doctrine of the Faith, once called Supreme, has now been downgraded to the rank of all other Vatican offices, while the pope's Alms Office has been inserted into the list before the Congregation for Divine Worship. The central idea is that it is not the doctrine of the Faith that evangelizes, but rather a "pastoral conversion," which now streamlines the bureaucratic structures, allowing the mission to be lighter, that is, less rigid, less dogmatic, in a certain sense more fluid and therefore adaptable to individual cases. Pastoral care dictates the doctrinal agenda of the Church's mission with the danger, however, of the mission itself becoming an exodus process, historical but above all political.

---

[143] According to Angelo Vincenzo Zani, "La responsabilità della teologia per una Chiesa 'in uscita,'" in *Teologia* 42 (2017): 3–22, the "Church that goes forth" basically concerns three things: (1) the interpretation of the Second Vatican Council; (2) the link between the evangelizing mission and the reform of the Church; (3) the coming into being of the doctrinal body within the pastoral body.

[144] See his interview of May 6, 2019, given to the German newspaper *Passauer Neue Presse*: "Kardinal Müller zu Machen der Kurienreform: 'Theologische Ahnungslosigkeit.'"

"The Outgoing Church" or Going Out of the Church?

If conversion entails going forth to a new Church, the result will be a man-made church and no longer the Church revealed by God in Christ through the Holy Spirit. However, people have begun to notice this and are not following. They are distancing themselves from the Church and the churches are being emptied. Yet one thing is crystal clear: there can never be a new Church. There has been a lot of talk lately, coming from various quarters, about there being a "new Church." This is incorrect. The Church is still herself and always will be one, holy, catholic, and apostolic. At most, there might be a caricature of it, an anti-Church, which wages war on the mystery instituted by Christ in a hierarchical mode with the Apostles and their successors. We should take these dangers into account, so that the one Church of Christ, the Catholic Church, encouraged by Pope Francis's exhortation to always be missionary, may free itself from the danger of being self-referential and may come to realize that only in Christ and in the Church's perennial Tradition is true renewal possible. If we know where we are going and why we are going there, we will also know why we are going forth.

5

Not Development but Doctrinal "Progress"— by Leaps and Bounds

On May 11, 2018, the Holy Father, in an audience granted to the Prefect of the Congregation for the Doctrine of the Faith, approved a new version of no. 2267 of the Catechism of the Catholic Church, concerning the doctrine on the death penalty. With this rescript, the new teaching entered into force on the same day as its publication in *L'Osservatore Romano*, August 1, 2018.[145]

The pontifical rescript affirms first of all that "recourse to the death penalty on the part of legitimate authority, following a fair trial, was long considered an appropriate response to the gravity of certain crimes and an acceptable, albeit extreme, means of safeguarding the common good." It does not specify what "for a long time" means; in truth, it is not only a chronological but also a *kairological* time: Sacred Scripture offers a clear foundation for this teaching, present in the Church Fathers and repeated by the constant Magisterium of the Church. We will not dwell on this but refer the reader to an exhaustive article, which explains this doctrinal development well.[146]

---

[145] For the Pontifical Rescript and the Letter to the Bishops of the CDF, see: https://press.vatican.va/content/salastampa/it/bollettino/pubblico/2018/08/02/0556.pdf.

[146] Cyrille Dounot, "Une solution de continuité doctrinale. Peine de mort et enseignement de l'Église," in *Catholica* 141 (2018): 46–73.

This "long time" has now come to an end, because, continues the rescript:

> Today, however, there is an increasing awareness that the dignity of the person is not lost even after the commission of very serious crimes. In addition, a new understanding has emerged of the significance of penal sanctions imposed by the state. Lastly, more effective systems of detention have been developed, which ensure the due protection of citizens but, at the same time, do not definitively deprive the guilty of the possibility of redemption.

This being the case, the new teaching is presented: "Consequently, the Church teaches, in the light of the Gospel, that 'the death penalty is inadmissible because it is an attack on the inviolability and dignity of the person and she works with determination for its abolition worldwide."[147]

What is astonishing here is the manner of reasoning: premised upon a new chronological time, it is said that "the Church teaches in the light of the Gospel...." Nonetheless, in reality, the Church in this instance means simply one single speech by Francis against a constant doctrine, which obtained ever since the beginning of Christianity, starting with St. Peter (1 Pet 2:13–14) and continuing up to John Paul II[148] and the previous formulation of the Catechism. Even more surprising is the Letter to the Bishops of the CDF, which goes so far as to affirm that "the new revision of number 2267 of the Catechism of the Catholic Church, approved

---

[147] Pope Francis, Address to Participants in the Meeting promoted by the Pontifical Council for Promoting the New Evangelization, October 11, 2017, in *L'Osservatore Romano*, October 13, 2017, p. 5.

[148] See Dounot, "Une solution de continuité doctrinale," 56ff.

by Pope Francis, situates itself in continuity with the preceding Magisterium while bringing forth a coherent development of Catholic doctrine." Solely on the basis of the renewed awareness of the dignity of the human person, present especially in John Paul II's *Evangelium Vitæ*, as well as in some speeches by Benedict XVI (both of which aimed at eliminating the application *hic et nunc* of the death penalty, but not its moral liceity), it is asserted that what Francis has ordered is a "coherent development of Catholic doctrine." However, in reality, *Evangelium Vitæ* did not intend to abrogate the *ratio* of capital punishment, but only to show its inappropriateness in the present social context, while obviously specifying that the commandment "Thou shalt not kill" absolutely forbids the killing of an *innocent* person. However, here, the assertion of continuity rests solely upon the support of merely the two popes who preceded Francis, and this, in spite of the fact that his new teaching is not in logical alignment with their own teaching on the issue. Now, what about all the other popes? What has happened to Scripture—for example, to Romans 13:4?[149]

What, then, does "a coherent development of Catholic doctrine" mean? What we wish to bring to the reader's attention is the following: are we confronted in this case with development in the theological sense or rather with progress in the technical-scientific sense? Before reflecting on the scope of the concept of "development" in opposition to its counterfeit versions, it is important to briefly examine the thought of an author who, having recently returned to favor, is now riding a new wave of popularity,

---

[149] To the point that Card. Journet could write: "If the Gospel forbids States to apply the death penalty, then St. Paul himself betrayed the Gospel," *L'Église du Verbe incarné*, t. 1, *La hiérarchie apostolique* (Saint-Maurice: Édition Saint-Augustin, 1998), 575, cited in Dounot, "Une solution de continuité doctrinale," 46.

and can help us understand the structure of the CDF speech. The author is the French Jesuit Teilhard de Chardin (1881–1955).

Teilhard de Chardin adds a peculiarity all his own to Darwinian evolutionism, namely the union of matter and spirit in the evolutionary process. To put it more clearly, he presents the idea that matter, through a process of becoming, produces the spirit, because it thus comes closer and closer to perfection, which is hominization and finally Christification. For Teilhard de Chardin the "Spirit" (a word he writes with a capital letter, as he does for some technical concepts, such as "Evolution," "Cosmic Life," etc.) is the product of matter, "emerges within matter as its master,"[150] and is in fact precisely this "Spirit which now evolves."[151] We are not robbed of our soul through the inexorable process of material evolution, but, on the contrary, the energy that emanates from the evolutionary process is spiritualized; it advances towards the constitution of itself as freedom.

For Teilhard, freedom is the product of matter that evolves and becomes spiritual. Evolution therefore goes towards a future at the summit of which there will be the full revelation/transformation of the cosmic Christ. Once we arrive at the complete unity of the evolutionary process, Christ will reveal Himself as the Omega Point. At that point, man will be more than man, that is, what Teilhard de Chardin dubs the "ultra-human" will be established.

We can rest assured: the social and industrial system does not rob us of our soul, because the latter emanates from energies which are beneficial and increasingly spiritualized forces. And

---

[150] Pierre Teilhard de Chardin, *Writings in Time of War* (London: Collins, 1968), 78; original French edition: *Écrits du temps de la guerre* (1965).

[151] Ibid.

only if we reach the heart of the "Noosphere" (another key word in Teilhardian vocabulary) can we hope to attain the fullness of our humanity.[152] The Noosphere, according to Teilhard, is the terrestrial sphere of the thinking substance. The closer we approach it, the closer we approach the fullness of our humanity.

The man who busies himself solely with the search for Revelation remains lost in emptiness and uncertainty; worse still, this bustling pursuit extinguishes in him the sacred fire of the "Search" (another capitalized word).[153] Religion, which attempts to reject nature, appears to be something alien to mankind. Religion no longer delights in that life which continues to govern the bodies and souls of her baptized children.[154] These people, whom religion seeks to sanctify in a jealous way, are hearing another voice, that of Mother Earth who first nursed them. First Mother Earth, and then religion. The latter, if it wants to thrive, must remain faithful to the primordial calls of the first mother. Therefore, it is a religion which is natural, and in some way rises as a canticle of the earth.[155]

Moreover, Teilhard unites evolution with the Cross and Redemption, transforming the latter into a symbol of the arduous labor of evolution. According to traditional interpretations, suffering is first and foremost a punishment, an expiation. However,

---

[152] Pierre Teilhard de Chardin, *The Future of Man* (London: William Collins Sons & Co., 1964), 190–91; original French edition: *L'Avenir de L'Homme* (1959).

[153] Teilhard, *Writings in Time of War*, 83. See also 221: through an interweaving of material and spiritual forces, the world goes towards personalization, which is a necessity for the "Universe" (another word in capital letters).

[154] Teilhard, *Writings in Time of War*, 86.

[155] It is no coincidence that Francis's encyclical letter *Laudato Si'* no. 83 (footnote 53) cites Teilhard.

in Teilhard's Cosmic Life, contrary to this view, the main idea that is derived from suffering is that of *development*. Suffering "is primarily the consequence of a *work of development* and the price that has to be paid for it. Its effectiveness is that of an *effort*. Physical and moral evil are produced by the process of Becoming: everything that evolves has its own sufferings and commits its own faults. The Cross is the symbol of the *arduous labour of Evolution*—rather than the symbol of expiation."[156]

Prudently, what was then the Holy Office published a *Monitum* on the works of Teilhard, saying that in philosophical and theological matters they abound in ambiguities and even errors that offend against the Catholic faith. Meanwhile, on the other hand, the Pontifical Council for Culture, led by Cardinal Ravasi, during the plenary assembly held in Rome from 15 to 18 November 2017, asked, in a letter to the pope, for this *Monitum* to be revoked. The main argument of the letter is that the Holy Office's preoccupation "has simply been surpassed by reality, because our current knowledge about the origin of man and the Bible has gone beyond the polemics that form the basis of the *Monitum*."[157] As is clear, Teilhard's key principle, namely continuous and perfective evolutionism, has also been fully adopted by the Pontifical Council for Culture. According to Antonio Livi, who echoes the criticisms which had been formulated by Étienne Gilson, Teilhardian speculation leads to a materialistic panchristism "that interprets Christological dogma—centered on the salvific events of the Incarnation and Redemption—in terms absolutely incompatible

---

[156] Teilhard, *Writings in Time of War*, 71.
[157] "Sul 'monitum' del 1962 riguardante Teilhard de Chardin," www.cultura.va/content/dam/cultura/docs/comunicatistampa/CS-23nov10Teilhard.pdf.

with the essential contents of divine revelation."[158] This position is also confirmed by Manfred Hauke, who adds that the confusion between nature and grace in Teilhard favors secularization. The work of the French Jesuit, in Hauke's view, has a strong tendency to panpsychism and pantheism: Teilhard is one of the fathers of the New Age.[159]

From this brief analysis of Teilhardian ideas we can draw some food for thought about our own time, especially regarding the tendency toward an inexorably evolutive vision of Christian doctrine. Teilhard de Chardin says that evolution is a continuous, unstoppable process which, precisely in its flow, goes towards greater perfection, towards an Omega Point, Christ in all and for all. Evolution is necessary and its best product is always the final one, the most updated. The latest period, though ephemeral, is always an improvement upon the preceding one and the latest result unquestionably better. Destined to be surpassed as soon as possible by the flow of events and its interpretation, this flow, however, is the reason for everything. To not "go with the flow" means to willingly bring about one's own death or perhaps, in more theological terms, to abandon the mainstream. Teilhard's evolutionary (and interpretive) process therefore inexorably advances onward without ever looking back. What came beforehand was necessary only for the sake of what has come to be, and this, in turn, will give way to what is to come. When everything is reabsorbed into this idea of a cosmic Christ, or rather of a Christian "Cosmic Life" (the Omega Christ being the religious trait of a

---

[158] "Il pancristismo materialistico di Teilhard de Chardin," https://cooperatoresveritatis.files.wordpress.com/2015/04/il-pancristismo-materialistico-di-teilhard-de-chardin.pdf.

[159] See *Die Tagespost*, December 8, 2017.

process of matter, which moves towards intelligence and spirit, and thus towards God), the process will cease and hence only then might this process of becoming be assuaged.

This notion appears to be quite widespread today, and quite popular in the Church among prelates and theologians. What is newer is always better. It is not simply the pursuit of novelty that captivates, but rather the idea that in the new, in the present becoming, there is a better awareness. A new pope abrogates a previous papacy, abrogates a missal, establishes a new practice, inaugurates a new tradition, or rather a new way of understanding tradition. In other words, there is a continuity of *becoming*, rather than a continuity of *being*. Becoming precedes being and Heraclitus triumphs over Parmenides.

In reality, it is a question of making peace between Parmenides and Heraclitus, saying that being and becoming are both relevant, but that there is no becoming without being and that becoming is not the surpassing of being, but its development or its corruption. When we move from the metaphysical to the theological sphere, it is clear that there certainly cannot be a "becoming" understood as a mutation of substance, but only either a legitimate doctrinal development or a degeneration in matters of faith and morals. For there to be a true *development*, it must be organic, linear, faithful to its beginning in all subsequent phases; otherwise it would be an adulteration, a counterfeit of the original idea.

The work of St Vincent of Lérins, a Father of the Church, is particularly suitable in this situation. He is among those who have stated with stark precision when a truth can be considered part of the deposit of faith revealed by God. In his work *Commonitorium*, written in 427, four years before the Council of Ephesus (431), he indicates a very precise rule that fixes the terms of catholicity:

Not Development but Doctrinal "Progress"

In the Catholic Church itself, all possible care must be taken that we hold that faith which has been believed everywhere, always, by all. For that is truly and in the strictest sense "Catholic," which, as the name itself and the reason of the thing declare, comprehends all universally. This rule we shall observe if we follow universality, antiquity, consent.[160]

Specifically in his instruction about the reality of *consent* (the *quod ab omnibus creditum est*), St. Vincent tells us that at least "all priests and doctors" must be in agreement. It is certainly not a material unanimity but a moral one, seen in the perspective of the adherence of all to the faith that precedes this same consensus. Faith, precisely by preceding consent, establishes it in a firm way. Faith comes before consensus in the Church. This consensus is therefore not simply aimed at seeking the adherence of a majority, even if defined as collegial. The adherence that creates consensus is given by the act of faith in the doctrine taught by virtue of its being proposed *always* and *everywhere*. Always, that is, from the Apostles onwards; everywhere, that is, in all the Churches where the same Gospel has been proclaimed. The union of *quod semper* and *quod ubique* understood in a diachronic way, so as to be linked through the Apostles to the Lord Jesus who came among us, facilitates the *quod ab omnibus*, unanimous consent. This is something to reflect on even more in our day when it seems that synodality is proposed as the foundation of ecclesiality and therefore universality. The synchronic moment is made to stand against the diachronic one and thus risks remaining isolated from the entire development of Christianity. Both of these moments are necessary, connected in that "everywhere, always, by all." Let us

---

[160] St. Vincent of Lérins, *Commonitorium*, 2.6.

say it once again: the "everyone" of today must be the "everyone" of always and everywhere. There is no need to convoke multiple synods to understand this; there is need simply to live in accordance with the *traditio fidei*.

St. Vincent of Lérins is echoed by Tertullian, who enunciates a similar principle that welds together the constant transmission of the Gospel and the apostolic succession: "*Quod apud multos unum invenitur, non est erratum sed traditum.*"[161] All that is unanimously maintained by the many Apostolic Churches, which have received the same Gospel, is not erroneous but transmitted. Where the many local churches preserve the unity of the faith transmitted, there is the Tradition of the Church. Therefore, where the geographical multiplicity of Churches preserves and teaches a different doctrine, the latter is no longer transmitted but erroneous: it is a corruption of doctrine.

This brings us to the present. Is the development attributed to the doctrine being taught—from *Amoris Lætitia* to the abolition of the doctrine of the death penalty—understandable from the point of view of St. Vincent of Lérins and Tertullian, or is it instead a matter of doctrinal leaps and bounds, at times involving discontinuous leaps rather than linear continuity? Should we not speak instead of doctrinal "progress" rather than of development? And here the term "progress" is understood in the sense of the Enlightenment: the commitment of reason to improve the personal and social life of man. In this way doctrinal progress echoes, in fact, the techno-scientific progress of development towards higher and more complex forms of life in order to achieve greater

---

[161] Tertullian, *De præscriptione hæreticorum*, chap. 28. We contextualize this Tertullian principle in our comments on Tradition as the "rule of faith."

economic, political, and social freedom. Is it not true that the new formulation of the Catechism, changing the teaching on the death penalty, hinges above all on a renewed social awareness of the dignity of the human person? What does this renewal consist in if, up until John Paul II, the liceity of capital punishment (and therefore admissibility, even if *in extremis*) had always been taught? Evidently the new cultural paradigm (Enlightenment) is what underlies the whole system. Above all, the new concept of punishment (only medicinal), which cancels and nullifies the other two aspects (vindictive and exemplary), borrowed from the Enlightenment thinker Cesare Beccaria (and followed by the utilitarian Jeremy Bentham),[162] rather than from the canonical and theological tradition, puts in place a new personalist, and no longer essentialist, approach to the death penalty.

We need a theological concept which again clearly specifies what development is and what, in contrast, alteration is—that is, progress understood as the accommodation of religious ideas to the standards of technical and scientific advancement. The following quotation from John Henry Newman's famous work can assist us in this regard:

> The highest and most wonderful truths, though communicated to the world once for all by means of inspired teachers, could not be comprehended all at once by the recipients, but, as being received and transmitted by minds not inspired and through media which were human, have required only the longer time and deeper thought for their full elucidation.[163]

---

[162] See Dounot, "Une solution de continuité doctrinale," 71.
[163] John Henry Newman, *An Essay on the Development of Christian Doctrine* (London: James Toovey, 1845), 27.

"Unity in type, characteristic as it is of faithful development": by "type" Newman means the external expression of an idea.[164] The unity or preservation of the type refers to the fact that, even when the external expression of an idea may change, the idea always remains the same, otherwise this would entail its corruption. Let us limit ourselves to the following question: is there preservation of the same type in the doctrine on the death penalty between the previous Catechism and its new formulation? No, because it is contradictory to affirm that it has now, out of the blue, become inadmissible, whereas Scripture, Tradition, and the Magisterium are in unanimous agreement to the contrary. If this were not the case, it would have been impossible to arrive even at its penultimate formulation: affirming that its legitimacy (and therefore its admissibility, even if only as *extrema ratio*) is founded upon the natural moral law, which is the expression of the divine law. To put it in Newman's terminology, we should say that we are faced with the corruption of a doctrine and not with its development.

How ought we to react to this distorted way of teaching Catholic doctrine? There is only one way: to return to the truth of the *traditio apostolica*, to rediscover its indispensable function for the Faith and its axiological value for theology. A faith and a theology without tradition are like that blind man in the Gospel, who claims to be guiding another blind man (cf. Lk 6:39). We would like to close these reflections with a thought by St. John Henry Newman: "Our popular religion scarcely recognizes the fact of the twelve long ages which lie between the Councils of Nicaea

---

[164] Newman, 58. Alongside this first fundamental "note" for probing true development, distinguishing it from the corruption of an idea, Newman enumerates six others: continuity of principles, power of assimilation, logical sequence, anticipation of its future, conservative action, perennial vigor.

and Trent, except as affording one or two passages to illustrate its wild interpretations of certain prophesies of St. Paul and St. John."[165] How many years have passed for our popular religion between the end of the Second Vatican Council and 2023? And are we really sure that chronological time is always better?

---

[165] Newman, 5.

6

Brothers without a Father
Because Deprived of the Son

The last encyclical of Pope Francis, signed on October 3, 2020, the eve of the feast of the Seraphic Father, St. Francis, bears the title *Fratelli Tutti*. This title is taken from the *Admonitions* of the *Poverello* of Assisi. It comes from the sixth admonition which, in its entirety, reads as follows:

> Let us all, brothers, consider the Good Shepherd who to save His sheep (cf. Jn 10:11; Eph 12:2) bore the suffering of the Cross. The sheep of the Lord followed Him in tribulation, persecution, and shame (cf. Jn 10:4), in hunger and thirst (cf. Rom 8:35), in infirmity and temptations and in all other ways; and for these things they have received everlasting life from the Lord. Wherefore it is a great shame for us, the servants of God, that, whereas the Saints have practiced works, we should expect to receive honor and glory for reading and preaching the same.[166]

---

[166] St. Francis of Assisi, *Admonitions*, 6, in *Fonti Francescane: Scritti e biografie di san Francesco d'Assisi, Cronache e altre testimonianze del primo secolo francescano; Scritti e biografie di santa Chiara d'Assisi*, ed. Ernesto Caroli (Padua: Edizioni Messaggero Padova, 1996), no. 155.

Extracting two words from an entire admonition to employ them in support of a discourse on universal fraternity—a discourse which in fact disregards God and His Son, the Good Shepherd, who, to make us truly brothers and children of God, underwent the Passion and the Cross—would seem to be a daunting task indeed. Yet Pope Francis aims to do just that, and ventures, by summoning the aid of the *Poverello*, to address all men. It is undoubtedly commendable to hope that one day men will unite in common values, renounce selfishness and injustice, forego waging war, and abandon the lust for power which reduces God's holy creation to a consumer wasteland. However, one cannot ignore the reality of original sin, which has deeply wounded man both in himself as well as in his relationship with God, and therefore, with the whole of creation. Yet there is no reference to original sin in the papal document, nor to the notion of salvation in Christ, who, by dying for us, reconciled us with the Father, and thus restored the conditions for reconciliation between all men. The desire to create a new, fraternal, and reconciled world apart from God and His Son, Jesus Christ, is yet another false promise of the ancient serpent of Genesis: you will be like gods, you will choose—instead of God and without Him—what is good and what is evil. Your life is in your own hands. That promise, however, turned out to be empty and ruinous from the start. The man, Adam, who opted for this do-it-yourself approach, did not establish, along with his descendants, a closely knit and happily united human family. The egotism inherent in the sin of disobedience to God has inclined him instead to a universal, fundamental, and destructive selfishness.

Revolutions and wars have been fomented which, even when waged in the name of humanity, freedom, or for liberty from hunger and alienation, have destroyed lives, have wounded humanity. The encyclical *Fratelli Tutti* seems specifically to overlook this fact, and with a desire more idealistic than realistic, proposes a novel way to reach this goal: namely, the good sentiments present in people, beyond religion, beyond and without the *religio vera*, without God. Religious discourse, though serving as a backdrop, is to be quietly surpassed, so it seems, for a more encompassing religion, that of fraternal goodness—one without the dogmas or doctrinal demands which are the source of mutual mistrust and religious conflict. This is a mere dream. It not only appears utopian (since, as we have said, no revolution fomented in the name of man has ever worked), but first and foremost appears to be Antichristic, as it excludes Jesus Christ. And it is all the more striking that it is neither a political leader nor the president of some nation who is speaking this way, but the pope himself.

Someone might very well object that the intention of the encyclical is to reach out to all men, to prompt men to dialogue regardless of their beliefs or convictions. It would therefore constitute an act of benevolence in a secularized way, marked mostly, however, by religious indifference. In truth, we must remember that the Church's mission has never been, and can never be, that of establishing a merely fraternal dialogue among people and ensuring that they converse peacefully with one another. While the Holy See's diplomatic mission to promote peace among peoples and States is laudable and necessary, it does not replace the Church's essential mission, which is to proclaim the Gospel of salvation in the name of the Triune God. The diplomatic mission of the Holy See is at the service of the Church's mission and not the other way around.

Unfortunately, it is the concept of "mission"—following Francis's understanding of the term—which thinly veils the assumptions that are putting a halt on the Church's mission. The "outgoing

Church" is not a church that evangelizes and wins men to Christ and the Gospel for the sake of their eternal salvation; rather, it is a Church that sets aside her outworn "habits" from the past, one that goes beyond herself, beyond doctrine, to open up to a dialogue about a purely human salvation. An example of this is the phrase (or rather, the slogan) "No one is saved alone," taken up in *Fratelli Tutti* (cf. nos. 32 and 54) and made official during the extraordinary *Urbi et Orbi* prayer service at the height of the Covid-19 pandemic (March 27, 2020).[167] No one is saved . . . from what? What salvation is being spoken of? Certainly, Christian salvation is not intramundane and is not to be confused with human solidarity or, in terms of social doctrine, with social charity. While the latter is the effort of Christian love to penetrate the social spheres with justice and peace, the salvation that Jesus has brought us is eschatological, transcendent, in God for eternity. The vision of time starting from eternity is lacking in Francis's encyclical, and this deficiency has the result of shrinking the discourse to the here and now, to the moment in which we are living.

The magisterial value of *Fratelli Tutti*

The encyclical of Pope Francis "on fraternity and social friendship"—like his previous one, *Laudato Si'*—is presented as a letter written to all of humanity, "to all people of good will, regardless of their religious convictions" (no. 56), among whom believers may eventually also find their place. Perhaps God's Word, as is the case with the Parable of the Good Samaritan, can be explained in such a way as to find in it, not an evangelical example of love in Christ, but an evangelical foundation for a universal love without any religious connotations. In these last two encyclicals of Francis, a

---

[167] In *L'Osservatore Romano*, March 29, 2020, p. 10.

novel style of circular letter has been initiated, no longer as being primarily addressed "to bishops, priests and deacons, consecrated persons, lay faithful and all men of good will," but simply a letter addressed to all. This is clearly the case in the letter under discussion in this chapter, and this novelty grants the pope the liberty to express himself according to his vision of things and to his personal opinions.

The absence of a specific recipient within the Church, however, highlights a further problem: such freedom of expression fundamentally disregards the Revelation of the Church, Sacred Scripture, and Tradition, which, if anything, are utilized as tools to justify his own ideas. The *formal object* of an encyclical letter is therefore missing: God who reveals Himself and the faith that emanates from divine revelation, which distinguishes a pontifical encyclical from a mere missive, enabling it to be inscribed in the long line of an authentic and ordinary magisterium. Rather than among the pontifical encyclicals, *Fratelli Tutti* should be classified as one of Francis's personal letters.

Moreover, a completely horizontal view of brotherhood immediately catches the reader's attention. The word "brother" does not have a theological meaning, but a social one, although borrowed from a discourse revealing a theological-political vision of history. Instead, it is a discussion that aims to bring men together. The key word, "brothers," should denote the fact of being fellow offspring *begotten* by the Word of God and the apostolic preaching, as St. Paul clearly teaches, for instance, when writing to the community of Corinth (1 Cor 2:1ff.). Here, he reminds them of the world in which they were made Christians, not by the power of sophisticated statements or extravagant speeches, but by the power of the word of the Cross of Christ. One is a "brother," one becomes such, only *in Christ*; we are children of the Father and participants with Him and for Him in the divine adoptive filiation by means of Baptism. It is Christ, "his only Son" (Jn 3:16), who, in accordance with the Father's eternal plan, becomes "the first-born among many brethren" (Rom 8:29), that is, of those who, having been called, have accepted the Gospel and become Christians: "For those whom he foreknew he also predestined to be conformed to the image of his Son, in order that he might be the first-born among many brethren."

We are brothers because we are God's children. Only if we have one unique Father are we truly brothers. This implies not only our being created by God, but specifically being *begotten* as a "new creation" (2 Cor 5:17) in Christ through the grace of filial adoption. It is true that in a broader sense we can refer to our being brothers because, as men, we are created by God. The Old Testament contains this concept of God's fatherhood connected with the creation of men. As Isaiah says: "Yet, O Lord, thou art our Father; we are the clay, and thou art our potter; we are all the work of thy hand" (Is 64:8).

This idea about the creation of the children of God, however, is part of the religious and salvific vision of Israel, that is, it concerns a God who is not only creator, but also savior, because He liberated His people from slavery and death (see especially Deut 24:18, Ps 81:8). All the Gentiles created by YHWH will come and prostrate themselves before Him; this is the hope of the psalmist on several occasions (cf. Ps 86:9). Later, it is Isaiah who gathers in a profound unity the two fundamental characteristics of God—fatherhood, and salvation as an offering of redemption: "You, Lord, are our father, you have always called yourself our Redeemer" (Is 63:16).

This salvific fatherhood of God is fully revealed in the sending of His Son who became man in order to manifest the glory of the Father and, through His Cross, gather "into one the children of God who are scattered abroad" (Jn 11:52). The unity shattered by original sin and pride is re-formed in the Son, so that whoever possesses the Son, professing faith in Him, also possesses the Father, but whoever denies the Son and finds an alternative filiation-fraternity does not even possess the Father, has no God (cf. 1 Jn 2:23). "Any one who goes ahead and does not abide in the doctrine of Christ does not have God; he who abides in the doctrine has both the Father and the Son" (2 Jn 1:9).

This brief *excursus* on the theological significance of the term "brother," completely absent in *Fratelli Tutti*, once again argues for it not being an encyclical in the sense commonly attributed to a circular letter of the Supreme Pontiff. It is actually a strictly personal opinion of Francis. If one tries to analyze it from a theological point of view, with a distinction formulated in *Donum Veritatis* of the Congregation for the Doctrine of the Faith (no. 24), it would be an *intervention in the prudential order* on the current situation, not without shortcomings; moreover, one that is strongly questionable, not so much from the theological point of view (because the discourse lies beyond it) as from that of the theology of history and of history as such.

The Good Samaritan: a cross-figure of human brotherhood?

The key theological argument, apparently, founding the thesis of a universal fraternity/brotherhood, without necessarily starting from faith and Revelation, is the Gospel parable of the Good Samaritan (Lk 10:25–37). With the account that Francis gives, it acquires a dimension of areligious transversality to unite religions and non-believers in a common and foundational value, namely universal goodness and love. The question, however, that arises in this situation is the following: is the love of one's neighbor, which the parable proclaims, a merely human value or a good in itself? Is it a merely human good without any reference to God? Even if we understood the good as an object of the will (therefore in a rational and philosophical way, ignoring any theological discussion), it would not cease being linked to God, to the Good as such; otherwise it would no longer have any reason for existence (being what it is and thus needing to be put into practice). Moreover, the context of the parable is a teaching of the Lord concerning "eternal life" (as are all the Gospel words elucidating the concept of "Kingdom of God" or "Kingdom of Heaven"). Indeed, it is in response to the doctor of the law, who tries to test Jesus by challenging Him with the question: "Teacher, what shall I do to inherit eternal life?" (Lk 10:25), that Jesus relates the parable of the man who falls among thieves. In this context we come to understand, through the unfolding of the story, "who is my neighbor" (Lk 10:29).

The doctor of the Law had responded with exactitude to the words of Jesus. He had invited him to look to the Law (cf. Lk 10:26), uniting Deuteronomy (6:5) and Leviticus (19:18): "You shall love the Lord your God with all your heart, and with all your soul, and with all your strength, and with all your mind; and your neighbor as yourself" (Lk 10:27). But then, wanting to justify himself, he shifts the conversation to the muddled notion of "neighbor." In the Old Testament, neighbor designates one's compatriot, one who lives within the same geographical border. The foreigner also becomes one's neighbor to the extent that he lives in the midst of the People of God; he may celebrate the Passover and may also be prosecuted like anyone else for any crimes committed (cf. Num 9:14; Lev 17:10, 24:16). The Samaritan who stumbles upon the man beset by thieves was not Israel's neighbor, because, like his compatriots, he was a foreigner and typically unclean because of the diverse ethnic background of his people in the central region of Palestine. Therefore, the question was intended to pose a challenge to the Master. There was still operative a partial vision of neighbor, which can be overcome only in Jesus and through His love, which knows no geographical and ethnic boundaries.

The Good Samaritan, in reality, is Jesus Himself.[168] Through this parable, the Lord teaches us to be close to all men and not simply to identify, among the multitude, he "who is my neighbor." Consequently, it is in Christ that the concept of "neighbor" acquires a universal connotation. This is the case, moreover, with the mystery of the Redemption: He died for all so that all might be redeemed from evil and sin and brought back to God. Thus, all those who live might no longer for themselves but for Him who for their sake died and was raised (cf. Eph 1:7; 2 Cor 5:15).

There is no trace in the parable of the Good Samaritan of a merely human love, nor of an altruism with philanthropic traits; it contains the revelation of Christian love, of God's love put into practice (cf. 1 Jn 4:7). "Love is of God" (ibid.) because "God is love" (1 Jn 4:8). There is no anonymous, neutral, religiously indifferent love. Neither is such a love present in the Gospel, nor in the world, nor in the life of Christians who live in the world, since, if Christ died for all, "all have died" with Him (2 Cor 5:14), that is, all are redeemed by His Blood poured out for many (Mt

---

[168] With other Church Fathers, St. Augustine (*De verbis Domini sermones*, 37) identifies the Good Samaritan of the parable with Christ and the man beaten and left on the side of the road with Adam, source and symbol of humanity fallen into original sin.

26:28). (However, though Christ certainly shed His blood for all men, all are not necessarily included among the saved, unless they participate with good will and good works.) Though human love definitely exists, it, likewise, is neither anonymous nor all-inclusive. Love of man, of a particular man, if not redeemed by the love of Christ, remains nothing more than *eros* or, at best, ascends to the level of *philia*, but without being able to attain its plenitude and, in any case, without embracing all men. The parable of the Good Samaritan cannot, therefore, serve as a story of the *human* transversality of goodness. Goodness and love are indeed universal, but they have become so through Christ and Christianity, without boundaries of race, nation, language, and religion. It is Christ who gives Himself freely to all men. An areligious use of the parable is simply not permissible.

Furthermore, if the Gospel parables teach us to seek first "the Kingdom of God and his righteousness" and Christ, the center of divine Revelation and its fulness, then the "kingdom of God" or "God who reigns" in our midst (cf. Lk 17:21), in every parable, as in the one under discussion, can only have, as its central message, the revelation of God's love in Christ.[169] The Samaritan bends down to tend to that unclean foreigner, robbed by brigands, and left half-dead on the ground, as Christ does to Adam, mortally wounded by his original sin and his pride. Christ humbles Himself and draws near to each one of us, plundered of divine goods in that first Adam, wounded and left at the mercy of his own fate, of his own selfishness. The interpretation of the Church Fathers, which, while respecting the literal sense, privileges the

---

[169] See Joseph Ratzinger/Benedict XVI, *Jesus of Nazareth: From the Baptism in the Jordan to the Transfiguration* (London: Bloomsbury, 2007), 199.

allegorical meaning of this parable, is very timely and of great spiritual benefit,[170] yet it is completely ignored by the encyclical.

For Francis and *Fratelli Tutti*, this may be a premise, but it never surfaces in the text. Indeed, the text merely states that passers-by, who remain indifferent to the battered and weakened man, were "lacking in real concern for the common good" (no. 63). Thus, the parable seems to invite us to rediscover our vocation as citizens (cf. no. 66). And so, in keeping with a theme dear to Francis, from those cast by the wayside one eventually arrives at those who "go through life as an outcast" (cf. no. 68). Of the possibility that someone might be cast by the wayside of life due to sin against God, there is no hint. Borrowing political categories well-known to social movements, the text states that the wounded are "those of our own people and all the peoples of the earth" (no. 79). With a rather peculiar outlook, then, Francis argues that, in reality, the parable, if interpreted in a religious (evangelical) way, not only does not solve the most pressing problems of the common good and of brotherly love, but, on the contrary, could become a vehicle of religious hatred, which makes men instinctive enemies of one another. Indeed, he writes:

> In those who pass at a distance there is a detail that we cannot ignore: they were religious people. Moreover, they

---

[170] Since St. Irenaeus and Clement of Alexandria, the Fathers, and in particular St. Augustine, St. Ambrose, and St. John Chrysostom, have read our parable in a Christological and allegorical way, paying attention to every detail that alludes to the mystery of the Redemption. For an overview, see St. Thomas Aquinas, *Catena Aurea: Commentary on the Four Gospels*, vol. III, St. Luke (London: Baronius Press, 2017), 370–77; Bruno Moriconi, *Farsi prossimo: Meditazioni sulla parabola del Buon Samaritano* (Rome: Città Nuova, 2006), 83–86.

dedicated themselves to worshipping God: a priest and a Levite. This is worth special note: it indicates that believing in and worshipping God does not guarantee that you will live as God pleases. A person of faith may not be faithful to all that faith itself requires, and yet he may feel close to God and consider himself more worthy than others. Instead, there are ways of living the faith that foster openness of heart to one's brothers and sisters, and that will be the guarantee of authentic openness to God. (no. 74)

There is only one way to live the Faith, and that way is following what Christ taught us, putting into practice what He did. Wrong ways are abuses which must be rejected, but not to the extent of calling into question the truth that charity's sustenance must be faith in God and our adoration of Him. If not, love of neighbor is no longer charity, but merely altruism, a human love and nothing more. "Believing in and worshipping God does not guarantee that you will live as God pleases": a symptomatic expression. This happens when the Gospel is not lived. But it is the Gospel and the New Testament, as we have said, that tell us that charity towards God is reflected in charity towards one's neighbor. In this way, truth be told, Francis criticizes religion: it constitutes a danger since through it one may become indifferent towards others.

The central idea of the encyclical can thus be summarized as an essentially anti-religious vision. Although *Fratelli Tutti* praises religious fraternity, there is an insidious criticism of religion, as being incapable of building a bridge between men, thanks to a historical fanaticism and an inherent fundamentalism, as well as the belief in Christ as true God, though He alone can truly make all men brothers. Religion as such has become the object of strong criticism. This starts with David Hume's empiricism, opposing dogmatic religion in favor of the pure cult of the *Supreme Being*, and arrives at the Enlightenment and Immanuel Kant through a rationalization of religion, with a dominant ethical note. Then we come to the "masters of suspicion," Nietzsche, Marx, and Freud, according to whom religion is fundamentally an illusion. Religion thus has increasingly become viewed as an irrational superstition, whose origin, fundamentally, is fear. This fear grows and radicalizes in religions because the dogmatic-spiritual system of each excludes the other and seeks to sacrifice the others. Terrorism and Islamic fanaticism in particular accentuate this vision.[171]

Gnostic and esoteric thought, in turn, tries to soar higher and to overcome fear on the one hand, and on the other hand, the rational-ethical confinement of religion. It attempts to appreciate and embrace all religions in a broader principle, in a transcendent super-religion, in which everyone is welcomed and where shared values are no longer religious and dogmatic, but those of gnosis. In the Christian-esoteric sphere, there is an attempt to resolve everything in God. Since truth is not a matter of doctrine, in this view, but God Himself, some Christians also embrace the Hermetic tradition in order to unite everyone. This "Christian hermeticism" seeks to be nothing more than listening to *"the heartbeat of the spiritual life of humanity"* and "living as guardians of the life and common soul of religion, science and art."[172] The desire

---

[171] For an overview of religion and violence, see Ednan Aslan and Marcia Hermansen, eds., *Religion and Violence: Muslim and Christian Theological and Pedagogical Reflections* (Wiesbaden: Springer, 2017).

[172] Valentin Tomberg, *Meditation on the Tarot: A Journey into Christian Hermeticism* (New York: TarcherPerigree, 1985), 7; italics in original.

to overcome religion, since it is regarded as a hotbed of division, the desire to go beyond all in a harmonious syncretism, may also underlie this esoteric claim to a transcendent and unlimited unity.

In *Fratelli Tutti*, religion, by virtue of its precepts and rites, excludes those who do not believe and do not share its approach; at all events, it would be a hindrance and not an aid to dialogue. This explains why the Abu Dhabi declaration serves as a guideline for *Fratelli Tutti* (cf. no. 5), using an idea of religious dialogue based not on the truth of God and His Revelation, but on the hope of achieving brotherhood through a notion of the good as overcoming religion or at least going beyond its domain. In the Abu Dhabi declaration, the syncretistic idea of a God who wills all religions as He wills the differences of gender, language, and race between people,[173] leads to the project of universal brotherhood rooted in human values—namely, in the same "human fraternity, embracing all human beings, which unites them and renders them equal" (cf. no. 285, the final appeal of *Fratelli Tutti*, in which the Abu Dhabi Declaration is taken up). And, if this discourse still lacks clarity, Francis makes it crystal clear by stating: "Paradoxically, those who claim to be unbelievers can sometimes put God's will into practice better than believers" (no. 74). That clarifies the matter, indeed. This criticism of religion and Christianity appears

---

[173] No distinction being made between positive divine Will and divine permission, but pointing only to divine Wisdom, the document says: "The pluralism and the diversity of religions, colour, sex, race, and language are willed by God in His wisdom, through which He created human beings. This divine wisdom is the source from which the right to freedom of belief and the freedom to be different derives." This clearly can only lead to syncretism rather than religious freedom. See Document on Human Fraternity for World Peace and Living Together, Abu Dhabi (February 4, 2019), in *L'Osservatore Romano*, February 4–5, 2019, p. 7.

not so much veiled as insistent, with Catholics accused—by those whose way of thinking is what we would call "secular," by the various ideologies we have come to know in history—of not yet having succeeded in creating this universal brotherhood, longed-for since the dawn of time. These ideologies promise a new Eden on earth, but, in fact, have all miserably failed to live up to their promises. Gnostic and Masonic thought would be quite at home here.[174] If *Fratelli Tutti* promises this kind of "new humanity," it is doomed to the same failure.

Universal brotherhood *versus* the universality of Christianity

Let us consider the problem from another angle. *Fratelli Tutti* contains an attempt to concoct a new universality in the name of human fraternity, based on the (neutral) good of love or, more precisely, in the name of the "universal scope" of "fraternal love" (cf. no. 6). With scant reference to the Father of all, without whom there is no true fraternity (cf. no. 272), *Fratelli Tutti* points to the fact that, as human beings, we are all brothers and sisters (cf. no. 128). However, this "fraternity" stands *de facto* against any "universality," precisely to the extent that it tries to exclude Christ and the *religio vera*. The dream is doomed from the start. We yearn to forge a new and universal fraternity—but without the Son, without His new commandment that goes beyond the narrow confines of nationality and cultural identity, beyond the narrow constraints of the human ego. On closer inspection, universality

---

[174] See Paolo M. Siano, *Un manuale per conoscere la massoneria* (Frigento: Casa Mariana Editrice, 2012); idem, *La massoneria tra esoterismo, ritualità e simbolismo*, vol. 1 (Frigento: Casa Mariana Editrice, 2012).

is not a characteristic of fraternity (we become brothers by virtue of a *generation*), but of truth. It is the truth which, being objective, is recognizable by all: it is what is and, thus, what I can know, but only to the extent that I adapt myself to it and accept it. If I try to manipulate it, it is no longer identifiable as the truth, but becomes its counterfeit, its negation.

Christianity among all religions has always "claimed" to be the sole *religio*, not to discredit other religions, but precisely because of the truth. The God in whom we believe has revealed Himself, has shown His face. It is the Son who reveals the Father and who in His love "to the end" (Jn 13:1) enlarges human horizons to welcome a love that comes from on high, which is not of man, but of God, and leads back to Him. Christ's charity is the manifestation of His truth. Since truth is universal, for everyone, Christ, who is the Truth, is a manifestation of its universality. The truth of Christ is His being-for-all, the God of all, of the Jews and the Greeks, of slaves and freemen (cf. 1 Cor 12:13). In short, it is the God who is, the God who is love. This truth and this love of God are universal; they are the manifestation of the universality of Christianity. In the name of the *Logos*, who is recognizable by all, and with the help of the human *logos*, which soon became *dia-logos* for the proclamation of Christ, Christianity has claimed from its beginning to bring the world, "all peoples," back to the Father. Christians have always proclaimed the Gospel to all men because the Master, before ascending to heaven, said this exactly:

> All authority in heaven and on earth has been given to me. Go therefore and make disciples of all nations, baptizing them in the name of the Father and of the Son and of the Holy Spirit, teaching them to observe all that I have

commanded you; and lo, I am with you always, to the close of the age. (Mt 28:18–20)

Universality is thus the dominant characteristic of Christianity. The attempt to exchange terms, substituting "fraternity" for "Christianity" and "brotherly love" for "truth," in the hopes of fostering a "new universality," simply means denying Christ and all that He has done. We must have the courage to admit this and to denounce it. This novel approach also means reducing Christ only to a superior man, a sort of social Good Samaritan, who bears the burden of the less well-off peoples, exploited by the selfishness of a global economy. He is perhaps the best of men, but merely a man, no longer God, no longer the God-man. The premises and conclusions of the encyclical, even if not always explicitly and directly, move in this direction. Pastoral zeal now appears to have become a desire to confirm the world in its distance from Christ and its disbelief. One can easily slip into an attempt to create a parallel religion of brotherhood, without God and without religion—a new-world religion, which, while criticizing religion, rises above it, with a maieutic function of guiding all toward respect for all.

This attempt has always been desired in envy of the One who is the Son and who alone has the power to make us all truly brothers. *Fratelli Tutti* constitutes an unacceptable downgrading of Christ to a better man for a better society. Therefore, it cannot be accepted either as an encyclical in the proper sense, because there are no adequate premises, or even as a prudential judgment on the part of Pope Francis. A collection of mere personal opinions? Yes, but the history of this imminent future will reveal its viability, or not. Meanwhile, "let us all, brothers, consider the Good Shepherd who to save His sheep bore the suffering of the Cross."

7

Those "Perversely Compassionate Persons" Who Turn Mercy on Its Head

In recent years, we have become so kind and merciful as to absolve even Judas. The abyss of God's mercy has encountered the abyss of the traitor's sin. If deep calls to deep (cf. Ps 42 [41]), then that sin could not fail to be swallowed up by a "greater" abyss and forgotten. This idea certainly arouses scandal, but it is the "scandal of divine mercy." This is how mercy was presented by *L'Osservatore Romano* on April 1, 2021, Holy Thursday, discussing the enigmatic figure of Judas. On that day the Vatican newspaper published two pieces on Judas Iscariot without bothering to veil a marked hope in his salvation. The first was a painting by a French Catholic depicting a nude Jesus bending over Judas, who has been taken down from the tree of his torment, embracing him and offering him some final solace. The picture, as the editorial by Andrea Monda explains, is "the fruit of the meditations" of Pope Francis, compiled in his book *Our Father, Reflections on the Lord's Prayer* (2018). In this book, the Pontiff repeats again the opinion he had expressed on several occasions[175] concerning the

---

[175] See, for example, his homily on this subject, "Judas, where are you?," April 8, 2020, where reference is made to the column capital of Vézelay, already referred to previously as "proof" to justify at least one doubt about the eternal perdition of Judas. However, John

possible salvation of Judas. In particular, he draws inspiration, in a very personal interpretation, from one of the column capitals in the Basilica of Vézelay in France, which supposedly depicts Jesus as the Good Shepherd carrying a dead Judas on His shoulders, like a lost lamb in need of salvation.[176]

Certainly the Church has never engaged in any sort of "inverse canonization" by declaring that a soul is in hell, not even in the case of Judas, who is nonetheless designated, in all the passages related to him, as "the traitor."[177] Between not stating, through an

---

Paul II had already said that not even Judas's damnation can be spoken of with certainty and that the surest way in this matter is the silence of the Church (see the interview *Crossing the Threshold of Hope* [London: Jonathan Cape, 1994], 186), followed by Benedict XVI, who, at the General Audience of October 18, 2006, said that it is not for us to judge Judas's gesture by substituting ourselves for God who is infinitely merciful and just.

[176] A 2016 study by a specialist in medieval iconography, about this column capital, concludes that it would actually be a well-known miracle in the life of St. James of Compostela, *le pendu dépendu*: an innocent man hanged and saved by the intercession of the saint. See the study published online: http://benoit-et-moi.fr/2016/actualite/une-histoire-de-chapiteaux-iii.html.

[177] There would not have been the aforementioned papal overtures without the questionable position of Hans Urs von Balthasar, according to which the Church has never taught in a binding way that anyone is damned. So, according to this opinion, even if we do not know that everyone will be saved, we can *hope* that no one will be eternally damned. See *Dare We Hope "That All Men Be Saved"?* (San Francisco: Ignatius Press, 2014). In reality, one cannot hope against the faith and against the clear words of Jesus Christ concerning those who will go to eternal punishment (see, e.g., Mt 25:46), unless one means a non-theological hope. Balthasarian thought, although defended by various authors, not least by Jesuit Father Mucci ("L'inferno vuoto" in *La Civiltà Cattolica* [2008] II, 132–38), manifests its weakness because of its

official pronouncement, that Judas is in hell and stating that he is (probably) saved, there is a vast sea: a sea of weak thought, which dilutes the truth in a supposed charity. But let us be clear on one thing: the Church has never made a solemn pronouncement on the case of Judas, not because there had ever been doubts about the fate of this "son of perdition" (Jn 17:12),[178] but simply for the sake of fidelity to the power of the keys entrusted to Peter. This power does not concern the damned, but the saved and the Church (militant, suffering, and triumphant). And yet, Saint Peter, in the Acts of the Apostles, describing the death of Judas as the condemnation of a wicked man (cf. Acts 1:16–20 in relation to Wis 4:19), leaves no room for doubt about the question of his salvation, even *in extremis.*

In reality, absolving Judas means condemning Jesus again, and condemning Him with the same act as Judas. In any case,

---

dependence on Origen, as has been pointed out (Werner Löser, *Im Geiste des Origenes: Hans Urs von Balthasar als Interpret der Theologie der Kirchenväter* [Frankfurt: Knecht, 1976], 83), and borders on gnostic speculation, in the opinion of Walter Kasper (*Misericordia: Concetto fondamentale del vangelo—Chiave della vita* [Brescia: Queriniana, 2013], 165n97).

[178] See the *Roman Catechism* (1566), which expressly declares the damnation of Judas (see no. 216, in relation to the words of the consecration "for you and for many," where the "for you" is in reference to those present or to the disciples of Jesus except Judas, and nos. 241 and 273. See also the collect of the Holy Mass *in Coena Domini,* according to the Missal of 1962, in which Judas, who received the "penalty of his crime," is contrasted with the Good Thief, who received "the reward of his confession." The Lord, in his Passion, gave different retributions based on the merits of each. For more such texts, see Peter Kwasniewski, "Damned Lies: On the Destiny of Judas Iscariot," *Rorate Caeli,* March 30, 2015.

it means trying to absolve yourself and to justify your own sin. Evil is absolved and good is condemned. Judas's action nonetheless remains abhorrent and irreverent, yet the most radical evil was, in fact, his rejection of mercy, giving in to despair. It is precisely this sin against the Holy Spirit, namely despair, which St Catherine of Siena, heir to a previous tradition,[179] sees in Judas's final action—a sin greater than betrayal itself. The Lord revealed to the saint:

> This is that sin which is neither pardoned here nor there, because the soul would not be pardoned, depreciating My mercy. Therefore is this last sin graver to Me than all the other sins that the soul has committed. Wherefore the despair of Judas displeased Me more, and was more grave to My Son than was his betrayal of Him. So that they are reproved of this false judgment, which is to have held their sin to be greater than My mercy, and, on that account, are they punished with the devils, and eternally tortured with them.[180]

---

[179] See, e.g., St. Thomas Aquinas, *In IV Sententiarum*, d. 46, q. 1, a. 2, qa. 2, ad 3; *De veritate*, q. 6, art. 2, obj. 11. Among the Fathers, see in particular St Leo the Great, *Sermo 62, De Passione Domini XI* (Judas might have been saved if he had not hastened to hang himself) and St Augustine, *De civitate Dei*, lib. 1, c. 17 (Judas despairs of God's mercy and thus increases his condemnation, leaving no room for salvific repentance).

[180] St. Catherine of Siena, *The Dialogue of the Seraphic Virgin Catherine of Siena, A Treatise of Divine Providence*, ch. 37. St. Veronica in a vision of hell, experienced on January 17, 1716, saw Judas with other despairing souls, forming the cushion of Satan's seat: St. Veronica Giuliani, *Un tesoro nascosto. Diario*, vol. III (Città di Castello: Monastero delle Cappuccine, 1973), 1006–8.

Believing "their sin to be greater than My mercy": is this not, especially, what happens when one persists in *doing* evil, transforming "justice" into mere self-interest, while remaining oblivious to the fact that mercy, in this case, is being used only as a temporary expedient? Jesus Himself, and faith in Him, are condemned by an iniquitous "justice" when mercy is completely divorced from it. In fact, the problem with the various contemporary merciful absolutions is precisely a mercy separated from justice, which rises up against it and attempts to annul it. In truth, a mercy that rejects justice also rejects itself. It has no *raison d'être* and easily becomes a caricature of the ideology of universal absolution. And this ideology is basically nothing more than a masked vigilantism. It is no mere coincidence that the pendulum often swings between profuse pardons going for a song, and intransigent executions without the slightest compassion.

The problem resides in understanding the nature of mercy, in spite of the attempt to exchange it for charity (or goodness) so that it is unceasing, boundless, and self-serving. However, this approach includes an attempt to represent mercy as an "essential attribute" of God and no longer as an attribute of God with respect to us (*quoad nos*), viewing it as what God is in Himself rather than what He does for us. Thanks to a theological stratagem, which has met with great success, Cardinal Kasper (heir to the thought of Hans Urs von Balthasar and his opposition to the knowledge of a hell populated with souls) thus attempts to reverse things in order to be able to declare "mercy for all," based on the fact that God's justice is only comprehensible on the basis of mercy.[181] The

---

[181] See Kasper, *Misericordia*, 140–99. See also my critical review, "La misericordia secondo il Card. W. Kasper," in *Fides Catholica* 1 (2016): 185–89.

main idea underlying this system is that mercy is God in Himself, a mirror of the Trinity because God is charity.

However, mercy and charity are not identical, they are two distinct virtues. Goodness and charity go together and are intrinsic to God, whereas mercy is extrinsic. Just as God's goodness is an essential attribute, equal to justice and knowable by natural reason, so charity is the very nature of God revealed in Holy Scripture (cf. 1 Jn 4:8, 16). Both goodness and charity belong to God as such, but mercy is God's action towards us. The latter is indeed an attribute of God, but not essential (it does not belong to His essence); mercy depends on God's goodness and charity, and is the manifestation *ad extra* of divine goodness and charity. Mercy, therefore, which is essentially "giving one's heart to the wretched," can never be *stricto sensu* a self-indulgent love directed towards oneself, but only a merciful love directed towards those who are in moral misery because of sin committed, or who suffer from material misery. Sin, which in itself provokes a punishment in those who commit it, also elicits our compassion towards those who have thus fallen, but it elicits *in primis* God's compassion. Here is the origin of mercy, which therefore has evil as its cause, as Aquinas explains.[182] According to Blessed John Duns Scotus, mercy, insofar as it inclines to passion, is not in God. This is seen mainly from the word, *misericors*, meaning merciful, compassionate towards the misery of others (*compatiens miseriæ alienæ*).[183] In the opinion of the Subtle Doctor, therefore, mercy is not in God, who is supremely just, but is a need on the part of the creature.[184]

---

[182] See St. Thomas, *Summa theologiæ*, II-II, q. 30, a. 1.
[183] See Bl. John Duns Scotus, *Ordinatio* IV, d. 46, q. 2, a. 2.
[184] Scotus, *Ordinatio* IV, d. 46, q. 3, a. 2. Scotus also adds that mercy and justice are truly distinct, and not simply from the point of

Hence also the fact that mercy depends upon justice and not the contrary. We will return to this point very soon.

The essential difference between charity and mercy lies in the fact that, while God is charity in Himself (and thus God, by communicating Himself to us, renders us capable of loving, through the gift of His grace and love), mercy, on the other hand, is charity granted as reconciliation and forgiveness. Mercy is love that heals us and restores to us the holiness which we had lost due to sin. Mercy, says St. Bonaventure, is commonly understood as "beneficence in the supererogation of goodness" (*benignitas in supererogatione bonorum*).[185] In charity there is the gift of God to Himself, in the communion of the Three Divine Persons, whose superabundance has been shared with us, through the gift of the Son and His Redemption. In God's mercy, however, two elements always converge: compassion (*rahamim*) and fidelity (*hesed*) towards His people (cf. Hos 2:21 in relation to Lk 1:78). If God were merciful in Himself, He would have to show compassion toward Himself and forgive Himself by Himself, and so sin would be rooted in God Himself. It would be blasphemous to think this, even though Luther did precisely that, along with his followers, who adopt an erroneous interpretation of the Pauline passage: "For our sake he made him to be sin who knew no sin" (2 Cor 5:21). According to this view the Father would *blame* the

---

view of logic, owing to the fact that they cause distinct effects. The effect of mercy is to deliver from damnation without merit, while the effect of justice is to condemn where there is no merit, or to save by virtue of merit. Since a real distinction in the effects cannot depend on a distinction solely based in reason, it follows that mercy and justice are truly distinct and not merely logically: *Ordinatio* IV, d. 46, q. 2, b.c. 3.

[185] See St. Bonaventure, *Sententiarum* IV, d. 46, a. 2, q. 2, concl.

Son for the consequences of sin; in this way, they attempt to introduce the reality of sin into God, thus making mercy essential and omnipresent.

As a matter of fact, mercy presupposes, on God's part, His justice and His charity, while on the part of man, the gift of grace and of charity, with the latter presupposing faith (following the first justification effected by baptism, the gift of a justice that sanctifies us). Mercy, therefore, can never be automatic. Although God's love cannot be exhausted, man's response is necessary—the will to be reconciled with Him. Therefore, if mercy is charity granted to us, nonetheless it cannot be given blindly, without our having a sincere contrition for our sins. Moreover, mercy can never be a gift that covers sins, leaving us in an objective condition of disorder, while we declare ourselves forgiven, though with no need to transform our lives.

In his *Commentary on the Sentences*, St. Bonaventure wonders if mercy and truth are among the very works of God. He responds by saying that they certainly converge in the same divine works, while they diverge *in connotatis*, that is, not on account of the diversity of the works, but on account of differing conditions within the same works. While mercy is "abundance of divine goodness" (*divinæ bonitatis affluentia*), justice is "the fittingness of divine goodness" (*divinæ bonitatis condecentia*).[186] Therefore, according to the Seraphic Doctor, mercy and justice "are in the same works, as well as in all works, for (God) does everything by virtue of the abundance of His goodness and does nothing by virtue of the abundance of His goodness except that which befits His goodness."[187]

---

[186] See ibid.

[187] "Nam primo modo misericordia, divinæ bonitatis affluentia, et iustitia, divinæ bonitatis condecentia, sunt in eodem opere, ita

We can clearly see in this reflection, which he continues by specifying the other two ways in which mercy and justice concur, the distinction between the goodness of God in Himself and the goodness of God in the abundant outpouring of Himself as mercy, which operates along with justice. According to St. Thomas, mercy is the greatest virtue only in those who are greater than all others, having no one above themselves, namely, in God. In those who have others above them, the greatest virtue is charity. Hence, once again, mercy and charity are not identical. In fact, Aquinas comments, "Charity likens us to God by uniting us to Him in the bond of love: wherefore it surpasses mercy, which likens us to God as regards similarity of works."[188] John Paul II also highlights this distinction when he says: "In the eschatological fulfillment mercy will be revealed as love, while in the temporal phase, in human history, which is at the same time the history of sin and death, love must be revealed above all as mercy and also be actualized as mercy."[189]

Mercy is love, but love is not always mercy. If this distinction is not properly taken into account, justice and mercy come to be equated with one another. At the same time, they come to be detached from one another, no longer being interdependent, with mercy no longer resting on justice. If justice depended on mercy, as is commonly believed nowadays, the application of justice would be subject not to God's goodness but to man's misery. But this is rather the case with mercy. Justice, on this erroneous account,

---

quod in omni opere, quia omnia facit ex affluenti bonitate et nihil facit ex affluenti bonitate, nisi quod decet bonitatem suam" (ibid.).

[188] St. Thomas, *Summa theologiæ*, II-II, q. 30, a. 4, ad 3.

[189] John Paul II, encyclical letter *Dives in Misericordia*, November 30, 1980, chap. 8.

could easily lapse into injustice. However, God is supremely just even when He forgives the unjust and the wicked. He does not cause any harm to others by forgiving injustice, nor does He take anything away from one person in order to give it to another, but He draws from the infinite treasure of His love. It is God's superior justice that founds mercy. God is merciful because He is just and does good even to the unjust without taking anything away from justice. Mercy in turn goes beyond justice, and perfects it, but never eliminates it. It presupposes it, even if it is broader than justice and tempers its rigor. If mercy were to eliminate justice, this would be the beginning of a moral dissolution; likewise, if justice were to forget mercy, it would easily become a harsh virtue.

We should listen once again to the voice of a great doctor of the Church, Saint Anselm of Aosta (1033–1109), whose works are too easily shelved because of his supposedly "juridical" vision. However, if his ironclad argument is ignored, one ends up falling into the prevailing false beliefs about mercy. Let us consider a very relevant passage from the *Proslogion*, in which the Holy Bishop of Canterbury prays to God and asks Him the following question:

> Is Your mercy not then derived from Your justice? Do You not then spare the wicked because of justice? If so Lord, if it is so, teach me how it is so. Is it because it is just that You are so good that You cannot be conceived to be better, and that You act with so much power that You cannot be thought to be more powerful? For what is more just than this? This, however, would not be the case if You were good by way only of retribution and not by way of forgiveness, and if You made to be good those not yet good, and not also the wicked. In this way, then, it is just that You spare the wicked and make good men from

bad. . . . But, it is also just that You punish the wicked. For what is more just than that the good should receive good things and the bad receive bad things? How, then, is it just both that You punish the wicked and that You spare the wicked? Or do You with justice in one way punish the wicked and with justice in another way spare the wicked? For when You punish the wicked it is just, since it agrees with their merits; however, when You spare the wicked it is just, not because of their merits but because it is befitting to Your goodness. For in sparing the wicked You are just in relation to Yourself and not in relation to us, even as You are merciful in relation to us and not in relation to Yourself. Thus it is, as You are merciful (in saving us whom You might with justice lose) not because You experience any feeling, but because we experience the effect of Your mercy, so You are just not because You give us our due, but because You do what befits You as the supreme good. Thus, then, without inconsistency justly do You punish and justly do you pardon.[190]

God is just when He forgives as well as when He condemns. In both cases He is merciful because in both cases He is supremely just. And He is as just as He is supremely good. Justice and goodness, justice and charity, flow forth as an outpouring of compassion for man's miseries through the gift of mercy. This is a gift greater than any human misery and any injustice, but not to the extent of turning a blind eye to evil; it does not, in the name of mercy, consider evil a good and, unfortunately, good an

---

[190] St. Anselm, *Proslogion*, cc. 9–10, from Anselm of Canterbury, *The Major Works*, ed. by Brian Davies and G.R. Evans (Oxford: Oxford University Press, 2008), 92–93.

evil; sin in that misunderstanding would be "good" because there is mercy for it, and the good would seem to be, alas, a sin from which we would willingly free ourselves.

Let us now ponder the well-known polemic of St. Augustine in his work *The City of God* against "some of our own tenderhearted fellow Christians,"[191] that is, against Origen's followers who did not want to admit that the infinitely just Judge will judge some to be worthy of eternal Gehenna. Origen was the head of this school of thought which held there would be a final liberation from hell—even for the devil—after a certain period of time. Here is how Saint Augustine presents Origen's thought concerning the apocatastasis:

> In this matter, Origen[192] was so moved by pity as to think that even the Devil and his angels, after very severe and long-continued pains in proportion to their guilt, would be snatched from the flames to join the company of the holy angels. But Origen has rightly been reproved by the Church on more than one account. One was this view of liberation from hell. Among other condemned views was his idea of the ceaseless alternation of blessedness and misery and the unending revolutions of the wheel of the century which brought on these goings and returnings of one and the other. Actually, this system which seemed merciful to Origen ceases to be merciful, since it imposes on the saints real miseries and penalties and

---

[191] St. Augustine, *De civitate Dei*, lib. XXI,17; Eng. trans., *The City of God Books XVII–XXII*, vol. 24 of *The Fathers of the Church*, trans. Gerald G. Walsh, SJ, and Daniel J. Honan (Washington, DC: Catholic University of America Press, 1954), 378.

[192] See Origen, *De principiis* 1, 6.

substitutes for their true and certain joy of everlasting good, unclouded by any fears, a series of false and insecure beatitudes.[193]

Then, according to St. Augustine, there are others who err "out of a sense of human compassion," but do not dare to go so far as to feel mercy even for the devil, to the point of imagining his salvation. If one were to go even that far, one might seem to become still more merciful, yet one would be guilty of a serious fundamental error: wanting to be better than God and His wisdom. Note the Augustinian irony:

> Of an altogether different kind is the error of those who are moved by human sympathy to feel that the miseries of men condemned to hell must have an end. They are convinced that happiness will be eternal for all who, sooner or later, are freed from torments. If, however, such a view is good and true merely because it is merciful, then it will be better and truer in proportion to the extension of mercy. Suppose, then, we extend and deepen the well of this mercy to include the condemned angels and say that after many centuries, however protracted, they will finally be freed. For, why should that well keep flowing until all mankind is saved and then dry up when it comes to the angels? Those who are moved by mercy do not dare so to stretch their mercy far enough to save even Satan himself. If any should be so bold, his mercy, at best, would be greater than those who do not and, therefore, his theory should be truer. But the fact is that the more merciful the theory is,

[193] St. Augustine, *De civitate Dei*, lib. XXI,17, in *The City of God*, 378.

the more it contradicts the words of God and, therefore, the farther it is from the truth.[194]

In fact, the disciples of Origen in our time do not go that far and leave at least the devil in hell. For "those who are perversely compassionate,"[195] who turn mercy on its head, Saint Augustine quotes the Psalm (33:9): "Taste and see how sweet the Lord is," reminding them that God has disposed the abundance of His sweetness for those who hope in Him; this abundance is in the justice of God "which grace gives without respect to merits."[196]

The homily that Don Primo Mazzolari preached in 1958 on "our poor brother Judas" has aroused the enthusiasm of many, even Cardinal Martini and Pope Francis himself. Why? Because a bit of Judas, after all, is in each one of us when, by sinning, we betray the Lord. So "who are we to judge," much less to judge Judas? In truth, we should imitate Peter rather than Judas. There is a confusion here between evil that is chosen and embraced to the end, and evil that is washed away by repentance and forgiveness instead. Perhaps the theory of Don Mazzolari, so favored today, is fostered in order to suspend God's justice for an indefinite length of time, so as not to be bothered by it. Peter also betrayed the Lord but he repented, returned to Christ, and obtained mercy. Better to be Peter.

Who knows if John XXIII, when he opened the proceedings of the Second Vatican Council, realized the disruptive force of his words relating to the medicine of mercy that Mother Church preferred to use from now on, no longer wishing to wield the

---

[194] Augustine, *The City of God*, 378–79.

[195] Augustine, *De civitate Dei*, lib. XXI,24.5, in *The City of God*, 392.

[196] Ibid. See Serafino M. Lanzetta, *God's Abode with Man: The Mystery of Divine Grace* (Lincoln, NE: Os Justi Press, 2023).

weapons of rigor (and of justice).[197] Justice was thus separated from mercy in the history of the Church and her acts. Those words led to a theological reinterpretation of mercy as divorced from justice—a thing of no small import, given the history of the effects.

---

[197] See John XXIII, *Gaudet Mater Ecclesia*, Address for the Solemn Opening of the Second Vatican Council, October 11, 1962.

8

Francis's Second Vatican Council: An "Ecclesial and Pastoral Ecosystem"

Talk is often heard of the "Francis event," marking a new stage in the life and history of the Church. This obviously cannot be separated from a more fundamental fact, the "Vatican II event," which is viewed as a positive development.[198] Pope Francis has also been called the first pope thanks to whom the conflict of interpretation regarding conciliar hermeneutics has finally been resolved.[199] Surely this is a new way of seeing Vatican II—a new way that remains elusive and difficult to grasp. On the one hand, there is in Pope Francis's writings and speeches an anchoring in the magisterial texts of Vatican II, although more sporadically and limited to some central documents; on the other hand, one finds also a surpassing of the letter of the text in the name of the conciliar spirit, in the name of a symbolic bond Francis has established on the basis of his recollections of the Council or his aspirations toward a reform of the Church. In this symbolic bond lies the Bergoglian understanding of the conciliar texts,

---

[198] See Ghislain Lafont, *Piccolo saggio sul tempo di Papa Francesco* (Bologna: Edizioni Dehoniane, 2017), 15.

[199] See Piero Coda, *La Chiesa è il vangelo—Alle sorgenti della teologia di papa Francesco* (Vatican City: Libreria Editrice Vaticana, 2017), 59–60.

a sort of reinterpretation[200] that never aims to define its spirit. He offers a broad interpretation, like a wide-meshed net that allows a variety of meanings to slip through, so that there may be a renewal. Renewal signifies here, strictly speaking, a "process," which in turn implies movement, progress, change. The essence *is* the process, and the process expresses the Church or the Synod that the Church is called to become in the name of the Council. In this chapter we will try to grasp Francis's interpretative *modus* through his words and documents, but also through his silences, all of which may appear to neglect the conciliar teachings. Yet, in the end, they are a new way, perhaps the most convincing way, to portray Vatican II as both the supreme council of the Church and simultaneously a mere premise for achieving something else that surpasses the Council.

What Francis says about Vatican II

One of the first important references to the meaning of Vatican II is found in an interview by the first Jesuit pope granted to the magazine *Civiltà Cattolica*, published on September 19, 2013, exactly at the beginning of Francis's pontificate.[201] The interview,

---

[200] See Christoph Theobald, SJ, *Fraternità—Il nuovo stile della Chiesa secondo papa Francesco* (Magnano: Edizioni Qiqajon, 2016), 26. This book basically reproduces an article: "L'exhortation apostolique *Evangelii gaudium*. Esquisse d'une interprétation originale du Concile Vatican II," in *Revue Théologique de Louvain* 46 (2015): 321–40.

[201] In *Civiltà Cattolica* (2013) III, 449–77 and on the website of the magazine: www.laciviltacattolica.it/articolo/intervista-a-papa-francesco/. The full interview was published in English on the website of *America* magazine: www.americamagazine.org/faith/2013/09/30/big-heart-open-god-interview-pope-francis.

conducted by Fr. Antonio Spadaro SJ, was quite extensive. Fr. Spadaro makes an interesting comment when introducing a question about Vatican II:

> "What did the Second Vatican Council accomplish?" I ask. "What does it mean?" In light of his previous affirmations, I imagine that he will deliver a long and articulate response. Instead I get the impression that the pope simply considers the council an event that is not up for debate and that, as if to stress its fundamental importance, is not worth discussing at too great a length.

Here is Francis's response, in which his preoccupation with the *Vetus Ordo* emerges, almost as a threat to Vatican II[202] and its liturgical reform; this preoccupation, manifested immediately (and implemented with the deconstruction of the institute of the Franciscans of the Immaculate), has produced drastic consequences in our day, as we will see:

> Vatican II was a rereading of the Gospel in light of contemporary culture, Vatican II produced a renewal movement that simply comes from the same Gospel. Its fruits are enormous. Just recall the liturgy. The work of liturgical reform has been a service to the people as a rereading of

---

[202] In a private conversation with the Jesuits of Chile, on January 16, 2018, Francis returned to the theme of the Second Vatican Council, denouncing the resistance towards the Council within the Church, which he claims is aimed at "relativizing the Council, watering down the Council." And he added: "Historians say that it takes a century before a Council actually takes root. We are halfway there." Published online at: www.vatican.va/content/francesco/it/spe eches/2018/january/documents/papa-francesco_20180116_cile-santiagogesuiti.html.

the Gospel from a concrete historical situation. Yes, there are hermeneutics of continuity and discontinuity, but one thing is clear: the dynamic of reading the Gospel, actualizing its message for today—which was typical of Vatican II—is absolutely irreversible. Then there are particular issues, like the liturgy according to the *Vetus Ordo*. I think the decision of Pope Benedict [his decision of July 7, 2007, to allow a wider use of the Tridentine Mass] was prudent and motivated by the desire to help people who have this sensitivity. What is worrying, though, is the risk of the ideologization of the *Vetus Ordo*, its exploitation.

More doctrinal and textual references to Vatican II can be found in the programmatic document of Francis's pontificate, the Exhortation *Evangelii Gaudium*. Francis espouses the vision John XXIII presented in his opening speech to the Council, according to which the substance of the Faith is one thing and the way it is expressed is another.[203] He distinguishes between the substance of the Faith and its form of expression, which occurs mainly through language. Francis reiterates that "today's vast and rapid cultural changes demand that we constantly seek ways of expressing unchanging truths in a language which brings out their abiding newness."[204] Then, criticizing an excessive centralization of the Church's structures which, instead of facilitating its mission, hinders it, the pope recalled the provisions of *Lumen Gentium* 23. That text discusses the concrete

---

[203] "Est enim aliud ipsum depositum Fidei, seu veritates, quæ veneranda doctrina nostra continentur, aliud modus, quo eaedem enuntiantur." John XXIII, Allocution *Gaudet Mater Ecclesia*, October 11, 1962; *AAS* 54 (1962): 786. See Appendix below.

[204] Post-Synodal Exhortation *Evangelii Gaudium*, November 24, 2013, no. 41; *AAS* 105 (2013): 1037.

implementation of the sense of collegiality through the contribution of the Episcopal Conferences, and expresses the hope that these Episcopal Conferences will become "subjects of specific attributions, including genuine doctrinal authority."[205] Finally, the principle of the "hierarchy" of truths as specified in *Unitatis Redintegratio* 11 is rendered by the Argentine Pontiff thus: "All revealed truths derive from the same divine source and are to be believed with the same faith, yet some of them are more important for giving direct expression to the heart of the Gospel."[206] In reality, UR 11 speaks of an order or "hierarchy" (put in quotation marks in the text) of truths because of their varying linkage with the Christian faith; a link to be understood therefore in the light of the *analogia fidei* and not as a sort of greater or lesser quantity or significance. All truths as revealed are important, to the extent that, if you deny even one, you are no longer Catholic.

Another important document in which Francis refers to the Second Vatican Council's authority, affirming that "with the Council, the Church entered a new phase of her history" in which it became necessary to tear down "the walls which for too long had made the Church a kind of fortress," is the Bull of Indiction of the Extraordinary Jubilee of Mercy, *Misericordiæ Vultus*. Quoting the opening speech to the Council given by John XXIII along with the closing address of Paul VI (where the latter compared the work of the Sacred Synod to that of the Good Samaritan towards a wounded humanity), Francis says:

> I have chosen the date of 8 December because of its rich meaning in the recent history of the Church. In fact, I will open the Holy Door on the fiftieth anniversary of the

[205] *Evangelii Gaudium*, no. 32; *AAS* 105 (2013): 1033–34.
[206] *Evangelii Gaudium*, no. 36; *AAS* 105 (2013): 1035.

closing of the Second Vatican Ecumenical Council. The Church feels a great need to keep this event alive. With the Council, the Church entered a new phase of her history. The Council Fathers strongly perceived, as a true breath of the Holy Spirit, a need to talk about God to men and women of their time in a more accessible way. The walls which for too long had made the Church a kind of fortress were torn down and the time had come to proclaim the Gospel in a new way. It was a new phase of the same evangelization that had existed from the beginning. It was a fresh undertaking for all Christians to bear witness to their faith with greater enthusiasm and conviction. The Church sensed a responsibility to be a living sign of the Father's love in the world.[207]

The same theme was taken up by the pope again in his address to the Italian Theological Association, received in audience on December 29, 2017. There Francis asked theologians to always refer to the event of the Council, and

to receive it the name of "creative fidelity": in the awareness that in these fifty years there have been further changes, and in the confidence that the Gospel can continue to touch today's women and men too. Therefore I ask you to continue to remain faithful and anchored in your theological work, in the Council and in the capacity the Church has shown for being made fruitful by the perennial novelty of the Gospel of Christ . . .[208]

---

[207] Apostolic Letter *Misericordiæ Vultus*, April 11, 2015, no. 4; *AAS* 107 (2015): 401.
[208] Address to the Italian Theological Association, December 29, 2017; *AAS* 110 (2018): 79–80.

"Event" and "creative fidelity" are the fundamental hermeneutical directives of Pope Francis's conciliar vision. A great stress in this direction appears in his comment to journalists on the return flight from Abu Dhabi, where he had signed together with the Grand Imam of Al-Azhar the document on *Human Fraternity*. This document cleared the way for a religious syncretism, justified as the "wise will of God": all religions are willed by God.[209] The pope, proud of this outcome, armed himself with the authority of Vatican II, or better still, with its spirit. He said: "This I emphasize clearly. From the Catholic point of view, the document does not pull away one millimeter from Vatican II, which is even cited a few times. The document was made in the spirit of Vatican II."[210]

Recently, at the end of January 2021, in a rather dramatic, harsh, and scarcely merciful way, Pope Francis, welcoming the participants in the meeting promoted by the National Catechetical Office of the Italian Episcopal Conference, recalled the need to renew catechesis according to the indications of the Council, looking towards it with gratitude but in an exclusive manner. Francis presented an equation of the following type: for catechesis to be inspired (solely) by Vatican II, it is necessary to note that "the Council is the magisterium of the Church," and therefore either you accept it and you are in the Church, or you do not accept it and you are outside, you are no longer with the Church.

---

[209] See Document on Human Fraternity for World Peace and Living Together, Abu Dhabi (February 4, 2019), in *L'Osservatore Romano*, February 4–5, 2019, p. 7.

[210] Press conference on the return flight from Abu Dhabi, February 5, 2019, at: www.vatican.va/content/francesco/it/speeches/2019/february/documents/papa-francesco_20190205_emiratiarabivoloritorno.html.

Therefore, all catechesis, to be in accord with the Church, must be based on the magisterium of Vatican II. Here are his words:

This is magisterium: the Council is the magisterium of the Church. Either you are with the Church and therefore you follow the Council, and if you do not follow the Council or you interpret it in your own way, as you wish, you are not with the Church. We must be demanding and strict on this point. The Council should not be negotiated in order to have more of these. . . . No, the Council is as it is. And this problem that we are experiencing, of selectivity with respect to the Council, has been repeated throughout history with other Councils. It makes me think of a group of bishops who, after Vatican I, left, a group of lay people, groups, to continue the "true doctrine" that was not that of Vatican I: "We are the true Catholics." Today they ordain women. The strictest attitude, to guard the faith without the Magisterium of the Church, leads you to ruin. Please, no concessions to those who try to present a catechesis that does not agree with the Magisterium of the Church.[211]

Francis's "symbolic" bond with Vatican II

It is difficult to find in Pope Francis's magisterial documents attentive and verbatim references to the Second Vatican Council, even though the latter constitutes a true compass of his pontificate. For example, in his three encyclicals, except for *Lumen Fidei* (to which Benedict XVI contributed), in which there is a reference to Vatican II as a council of the Church (no. 6; no. 40 on

---

[211] Address to participants in the meeting promoted by the National Catechetical Office of the Italian Episcopal Conference, January 30, 2021, in *L'Osservatore Romano*, January 30, 2021, p. 12.

Apostolic Tradition), neither *Laudato Si'* nor *Fratelli Tutti* contain any references. Among the Post-Synodal Apostolic Exhortations, only *Evangelii Gaudium* and *Amoris Lætitia* have somewhat more frequent references to the texts of Vatican II; in the others, only here and there do we find some mention, more as embellishment than reference. Why such a scarcity of words? We have already found a first response in the comment made by Fr. Spadaro, in his first interview with Francis.

Another reason may be the fact that Francis is the first post-conciliar pontiff, someone who did not participate in Vatican II. His feelings and his work are situated exclusively in the receptive phase, with an interpretative vision of the reception itself. In fact, specifically in reference to the latter, there is the testimony of Andrea Riccardi, who, during the presentation in Rome of one of his books on the pope, on October 8, 2013, revealed a friendly exchange he had had with Francis. The founder of the Community of St. Egidio pointed out to the pope: "You do not talk much about the Council," to which he replied: "The Council needs to be put into action, rather than simply talked about."[212]

More recently, Pope Francis himself wrote the foreword to a book dedicated to him, *Siblings All, Sign of the Times: The Social Teaching of Pope Francis*.[213] There he explained the reasons for his

---

[212] The testimony is reported by Andrea Lebra, "Papa Francesco e il Vaticano II," on the website *SettimanaNews*, February 26, 2018, at www.settimana news.it/chiesa/papa-francesco-vaticano-ii/#_ftnref6; and also by Tommaso Stenico, *Il Concilio Vaticano II: Carisma e profezia* (Milan: Finoia, 2020), 59 (but without revealing Riccardi's name).

[213] Card. Michael Czerny and Christian Barone, *Siblings All, Sign of the Times: The Social Teaching of Pope Francis*, with a foreword by Pope Francis (Maryknoll, NY: Orbis Books, 2022).

being so sparing with words about the magisterium of Vatican II. How does it happen that this connection, which is so crucial, does not manifest itself? Here is Francis's response, thanking the book's authors who attempt to unearth this bond in *Fratelli Tutti*:

> In the history of Latin America, in which I have been immersed, first as a young Jesuit student and then in the exercise of the ministry, we breathe an ecclesial atmosphere that has absorbed enthusiastically and made its own the theological, ecclesial, and spiritual intuitions of the Council and has inculturated and applied them. For us, the younger ones, the Council became the horizon of our belief, of our languages, and of our praxis, that is, it soon became our ecclesial and pastoral ecosystem, but we didn't have the habit of frequently quoting the Conciliar Decrees or pausing in speculative reflections. The Council had simply entered our way of being Christians and of being Church and, in the course of life, my intuitions, perceptions, and spirituality were simply generated by the suggestions of Vatican II's doctrine. There was not much need to quote the Council's texts. Today, several decades having passed and finding ourselves in a profoundly changed world—also ecclesial—it's probably necessary to make more explicit the key concepts of Vatican Council II, the foundations of its arguments, its theological and pastoral horizon, and the arguments and the method it used.[214]

There is indeed a link with Vatican II, and a strong one at that. Though not expressed, it is present in the entire ministry

---

[214] Preface also published in *L'Osservatore Romano* on September 28, 2021, p. 8.

of Francis: it is his "ecclesial and pastoral ecosystem." Thus, it is basically a matter of interpreting this bond, of spotting it here and there, in some doctrinal item dear to the Pontiff's heart, as many have already attempted to do. Francis seeks to surpass the stalemate between a hermeneutic of continuity and a hermeneutic of rupture, trying to pick up the threads of a very complex event, bridging the gap (as it were) by eloquent silences and ambiguous words.[215]

Here are a few examples. A substantial link with the last council is recognizable in the concept of mercy so frequent in the teaching of Pope Francis. This seems to represents "a leap forward" in comparison with the conciliar teaching.[216] Moreover, Francis's idea or dream of a "poor Church for the poor" would be an echo of *Lumen Gentium* 8 which teaches, among other things, that precisely in the poor and suffering the Church recognizes the image of her founder, poor and suffering, and seeks to alleviate others' suffering.[217] Further, the sober style of Pope Francis, accompanied by his ecclesiological dream of poverty, and manifest in the name he chose, recalls the famous Pact of the Catacombs. With this agreement (dated November 16, 1965), some Latin American bishops, headed by Bishop Hélder Câmara, sought to seal their hermeneutic of Vatican II with the option for the poor. This returned to the agenda during the first Roman phase of the Synod on Synodality in October

---

[215] See Marinella Perroni, *Kerigma e profezia: L'ermeneutica biblica di papa Francesco* (Vatican City: Libreria Editrice Vaticana, 2017), 70.

[216] See Roberto Repole, *Il sogno di una Chiesa evangelica— L'ecclesiologia di Papa Francesco* (Vatican City: Libreria Editrice Vaticana, 2017), 31.

[217] See Repole, 43.

2023. Jorge Mario Bergoglio would embody that ideal first as bishop of Buenos Aires and then as bishop of Rome.[218] Even the concept of the Church as "the people of God," generally favored by Francis over other ecclesiological definitions, is seen as a distinct reference to Vatican II. For Francis, the Church as a people includes the totality of the baptized, whose dignity derives from baptism and the anointing of the Holy Spirit. Therefore, no group in the Church, neither clerics nor laity, can take the place of others by claiming to speak for the whole.[219] A Church that is the People of God, in which there is a common dignity and a fraternal equality in Christ, necessarily becomes a synodal Church: a journeying together of all, privileging the "bottom-up" dimension rather than a pyramidal hierarchy of a Church too cramped and constricting to welcome all. Of this prevalent synodality we can find no trace in Vatican II, as Francis has done, but in the opinion of Don Roberto Repole, the ecclesiology of the people of God and of the *sensus fidei* were its premises.[220]

Francis: the essence is the process

What it all comes down to is this: Vatican II and its texts serve merely as a premise in Pope Francis's teaching and in his firm resolution to reform the Church. Francis goes beyond the Council, far beyond. In my opinion, there are two themes which, more than any others, manifest the symbolic, non-textual anchoring of Francis to Vatican II and therefore his surpassing it—which is also predictable since he does not normally

---

[218] See Perroni, *Kerigma e profezia*, 73.
[219] See Repole, *Il sogno*, 59–61.
[220] See Repole, 109.

feel the need to refer to its texts. The two areas in question are synodality and liturgy.

The main link between synodality and the Council—above all the starting point—is to be sought in episcopal collegiality (cf. *Christus Dominus* no. 5). Collegiality and synodality are not the same thing, but Francis shows their close connection thusly:

> The last level is that of the universal Church. Here the Synod of Bishops, representing the Catholic episcopate, becomes an expression of *episcopal collegiality* within an entirely synodal Church. Two different phrases: "episcopal collegiality" and an "entirely synodal Church." This level manifests the *collegialitas affectiva*, which can also become in certain circumstances "effective," joining the bishops among themselves and with the pope in solicitude for the People God.[221]

The synod for Francis is a "program" of action aimed at making the Church entirely synodal, in which the "principle of synodality"[222] (echo of the "principle" or the "law of conciliarity"[223]) is applied, and it is ripe with ecumenical hopes. Synodality is seen "as a constitutive dimension of the Church" that "offers us the most appropriate interpretive framework for understanding the hierarchical ministry itself";[224] its theological seedbed is provided by the *sensus fidei*, a

---

[221] Address at the Commemorative Ceremony for the 50th Anniversary of the Institution of the Synod of Bishops, October 17, 2015; *AAS* 107 (2015): 1143.

[222] See Address to the Ecumenical Delegation of the Patriarchate of Constantinople, June 27, 2015, cited in the aforementioned Commemorative Ceremony: *AAS* 107 (2015): 1144.

[223] See Serafino M. Lanzetta, *Vatican II, A Pastoral Council: Hermeneutics of Council Teaching* (Leominster: Gracewing, 2016), 120–28.

[224] Commemorative Ceremony; *AAS* 107 (2015): 1141–42.

quality shared by all the baptized: "The *sensus fidei* prevents a rigid separation between an *Ecclesia docens* and an *Ecclesia discens*, since the flock likewise has an instinctive ability to discern the new ways that the Lord is revealing to the Church."[225] However, we should also remember that the *sensus fidei* is immediate adherence, by virtue of the grace of the Holy Spirit, to the faith of the Church and not a mere act of the believing subject, which, as such, would place all believers on an equal footing. The hierarchical Church, divinely constituted, precedes the *sensus fidei* of the faithful.

Additionally, the synodal process, in the Pontiff's opinion, must lead us to journey *"not occasionally but structurally* towards a *synodal Church*: an open square, where all can feel at home and participate."[226] The Church can thus avoid three risks: formalism (a beautiful façade without substance), intellectualism (conversing with one another through cultivated but abstract reasoning), and immobilism (refusing to change the *status quo* based on the attitude that says: "We have always done it this way").[227] The idea that the synod is the structure of the Church, making the Church what it is, was elucidated by Yves Congar, according to whom Vatican II had to express the "fundamental conciliarity" of the Church.[228] All this is meant to lead to a true reform that Pope

---

[225] Ibid., 1140.

[226] "Moment of Reflection for the Beginning of the Synodal Journey," in *L'Osservatore Romano*, October 9, 2021, p. 3.

[227] Ibid.

[228] See Yves Congar, "Konzils als Versammlung und grundsätzliche Konziliarität der Kirche," in J.B. Metz, W. Kern, A. Darlapp, H. Vorgrimler, eds., *Gott in Welt: Festgabe für Karl Rahner*, vol. II (Freiburg im Breisgau: Herder, 1964), 135–65, at 154–55; idem, "Note sul Concilio come assemble e sulla conciliarità fondamentale della Chiesa," in *Orizzonti attuali della teologia*, vol. II (Roma: Edizioni Paoline, 1967), 172–73.

Francis explains (not by chance) by citing the words of Congar: "There is no need to create *another church*, but to create a *different church*."[229] A different Church (different from the way her Head made it?), already modeled *in pectore* by Francis through a vision that is very close to the concept of revolution (turning again or turning back) or reversal of positions. He even finds inspiration in the *Magnificat* of the Blessed Virgin. The pope writes:

> Jesus founded the Church by setting at her head the Apostolic College, in which the Apostle Peter is the "rock" (cf. Mt 16:18), the one who must confirm his brethren in the faith (cf. Lk 22:32). But in this Church, as in an inverted pyramid, the top is located beneath the base. Consequently, those who exercise authority are called "ministers," because, in the original meaning of the word, they are the least of all.[230]

And he continues:

> There is a certain resistance to moving beyond the image of a Church rigidly divided into leaders and followers, those who teach and those who are taught; we forget that God likes to overturn things: as Mary said, "he has thrown down the rulers from their thrones but lifted up the lowly" (Lk 1:52). Journeying together tends to be more horizontal than vertical.[231]

---

229 *Vera e falsa riforma nella Chiesa* (Milan: Jaca Book, 1994), 193, cited in "Moment of Reflection," *L'Osservatore Romano*, October 9, 2021, p. 3.

230 Commemorative Ceremony; *AAS* 107 (2015): 1142.

231 Address to the Faithful of the Diocese of Rome, September 18, 2021, in *L'Osservatore Romano*, September 18, 2021, p. 3.

Finally, among the things in most urgent need of reform, according to Pope Francis, is the "conversion of the papacy":

> The pope is not, by himself, above the Church; but within it as one of the baptized, and within the College of Bishops as a Bishop among Bishops, called at the same time—as Successor of Peter—to lead the Church of Rome which presides in charity over all the Churches.[232]

Being inside the Church on the part of the pope, however, should mean believing with the faith of the Church, being obedient to her perennial *traditio*. Only in this way does the pope avoid bypassing the Church by placing himself above it, and become capable, with a servant's humility, of serving all those who believe in Christ and follow Him by good works. Only in this way does he also become capable of confirming his brethren. Instead, it seems that the pope and the Church must now think of something else, remaking the Church from its foundations, in the image and likeness of the Synod. Whether or not this is what the episcopal collegiality of *Lumen Gentium* was aiming at is hard to say. What is certain is that Vatican II has already been set aside.

Vatican II, the only expression of the Church's *lex orandi*

The idea of conciliarity, so widespread in the interventions of Pope Francis, more as a spirit than as a body of texts, shifts, however, into reverse gear when he demonstrates a marked preference for the letter of the Council as regards the liturgical sphere. At times it seems that the concept of a "militant Church" resurfaces, replaced by Vatican II with the word "pilgrim." The summer of 2021 saw a drastic intervention by the pope with a motu proprio

[232] Commemorative Ceremony; *AAS* 107 (2015): 1144.

entitled *traditionis Custodes*, which not only abolishes the previous one of Benedict XVI (*Summorum Pontificum*, thanks to which all priests were granted the faculty to celebrate Mass according to the Roman Missal of 1962 without any permission from the local Ordinary), but also lays plans for the disappearance of this same Mass, regarded as the enemy of unity, and now subject to strict bans and heavy restrictions. Among other things, what *traditionis Custodes* states in article 1 is particularly striking: "The liturgical books promulgated by Saint Paul VI and Saint John Paul II, in conformity with the decrees of Vatican Council II, are the unique expression of the *lex orandi* of the Roman Rite."[233]

But if this is so, why is it still possible for the bishops, when they deem it appropriate, to grant the faculty to celebrate according to the ancient Roman Missal, most recently updated by John XXIII? This would mean, according to the logic of the motu proprio, authorizing a Mass which does not express the *lex orandi* of the Church. What *does* it express then? And why should anyone be authorized to celebrate it? In reality, one cannot restrict the *lex orandi* to one particular part of the Church, the most up-to-date and most recent. Either the *lex orandi* expresses the whole Church (with all its councils and all its rites) in a symphonic unity, or it does not express it at all. On Francis's premise, bishops are acting rather as "soldiers" of a tradition that begins with the Council, and not as "guardians" of a *traditio* that begins with the Apostles, as befits their successors. The fact that Vatican II is the most recent council of the Church does not necessarily mean that it expresses the Church's whole *traditio* of faith and of

---

[233] Motu Proprio *Traditionis Custodes* on the Use of the Roman Liturgy Prior to the Reform of 1970, July 16, 2021, in *L'Osservatore Romano*, July 16, 2021, p. 2.

prayer—all the more so because the last council was positioned on an atypically pastoral level.[234] Moreover, the *ex abrupto* composition of a new Missal had not been anticipated, but at most, the updating of the previous one, as had always been the case in the past. Instead, the *postconciliar* reform resulted in two missals, the older of which had never been abrogated, as Benedict XVI declared with *Summorum Pontificum* (art. 1). For Francis, this was the most unacceptable thing about Pope Benedict in liturgical matters, for which he was never to be forgiven.

The *Letter* addressed to all the bishops with which Francis accompanied his motu proprio is also very significant. The magisterial and liturgical authority of Vatican II is present from the first line of this letter to the last. For example, the pope expresses himself in the following way to denounce the abuses of authority he asserts are being transmitted by the ancient Mass:

> I am nonetheless saddened that the instrumental use of [the] *Missale Romanum* of 1962 is often characterized by a rejection not only of the liturgical reform, but of the Vatican Council II itself, claiming, with unfounded and unsustainable assertions, that it betrayed the Tradition and the "true Church." The path of the Church must be seen within the dynamic of Tradition "which originates from the Apostles and progresses in the Church with the assistance of the Holy Spirit" (DV 8). A recent stage of this dynamic was constituted by Vatican Council II where the Catholic episcopate came together to listen and to discern the path

---

[234] Theologians have very different ideas about how to understand the pastorality of Vatican II. For a synthesis, see Lanzetta, *Vatican II, A Pastoral Council*, xlii–l; cf. Appendix below.

for the Church indicated by the Holy Spirit. To doubt the Council is to doubt the intentions of those very Fathers who exercised their collegial power in a solemn manner *cum Petro et sub Petro* in an ecumenical council, and, in the final analysis, to doubt the Holy Spirit himself who guides the Church.[235]

And he continues:

A final reason for my decision is this: ever more plain in the words and attitudes of many is the close connection between the choice of celebrations according to the liturgical books prior to Vatican Council II and the rejection of the Church and her institutions in the name of what is called the "true Church." One is dealing here with comportment that contradicts communion and nurtures the divisive tendency—"I belong to Paul; I belong instead to Apollo; I belong to Cephas; I belong to Christ"—against which the Apostle Paul so vigorously reacted. In defense of the unity of the Body of Christ, I am constrained to revoke the faculty granted by my Predecessors. The distorted use that has been made of this faculty is contrary to the intentions that led to granting the freedom to celebrate the Mass with the *Missale Romanum* of 1962.[236]

On what basis can it be affirmed that the ancient Missal fostered hostility to Vatican II and division within the Church? There

---

[235] Letter to the Bishops of the Whole World, that Accompanies the Apostolic Letter Motu Proprio *Traditionis Custodes* on the Use of the Roman Liturgy Prior to the Reform of 1970, July 16, 2021, published in *L'Osservatore Romano* on July 16, 2021, p. 3.
[236] Ibid.

are liturgical theses that lean towards this line of reasoning,[237] but a pope's observations should be substantiated by dogmatically, morally, and liturgically relevant *facts*, known to all. Certainly, the blogosphere might also have influenced this conclusion, but this should remain irrelevant when it comes to making such an important decision, so rife with consequences.

What is certain, however, is that the Second Vatican Council, which risks being sidelined by a synodality with a "bottom-up" structure, or in any case becoming a mere launching pad, has largely recuperated, thanks to *Traditionis Custodes*, its liturgical authority. However, this is disconnected from the intricacy of the *lex credendi*, which is the *lex orandi* of the entire Church. In this way the following words uttered by Francis resound with prophetic power: "the liturgical reform is irreversible."[238] Here we see a sort of dogmatization of a certain interpretation and application of *Sacrosanctum Concilium*—one whose effects his predecessors themselves had sought to alleviate.

---

[237] It seems that the theologian who conceived *Traditionis Custodes*, or at least the one whose ideas come closest to it, is Andrea Grillo, according to whom *Summorum Pontificum* would have introduced a "state of exception" destined to be overcome by giving full and exclusive authority back to Vatican II, through which the true liturgical reconciliation had taken place: "Superare lo stato di eccezione liturgica: restituire autorita alla *lex orandi* e ai vescovi," in A. Grillo and Z. Carra, eds., *Oltre "Summorum Pontificum": Per una riconciliazione liturgica possibile* (Bologna: EDB, 2020), 67–76. See Peter Kwasniewski, "Andrea Grillo: The Mind Behind the Motu Proprio," *OnePeterFive*, August 18, 2021, and other articles on Grillo by the same author at the same website.

[238] Address to Participants in the 68th National Liturgical Week in Italy, August 24, 2017.

Conclusion

What emerges from this *excursus* on Francis's way of understanding and interpreting Vatican II is the partialness of usage, dependent upon the situation one is confronted with, and the fruit of a new hermeneutic (more theological than magisterial), on the part of the first pope who did not participate in the Council. If Benedict XVI's categories of hermeneutics of continuity or rupture could still be used, Francis's hermeneutic would be identified as a rupture and a new beginning, openly favoring certain theological theses that go in this direction. But even Benedict XVI's categories would be insufficient to encompass the phenomenon or perhaps can no longer be proposed. Francis has his own way of referring to the Council, which is textual in some cases, very sporadically, but above all, symbolic, based on the idea of the Council as an "event," which can also be defined as the "principle of conciliarity." Everything is conciliar, even the absence of references to the Council documents, because that assembly was in any case only a premise for a further development—or rather, for a permanent structural process for the sake of carrying out a profound reform of the Church. In fact, it is a remaking of the Church as *odós*: the pathway of all and for all, without, however, this new missionary spirit necessarily meaning the leading of the Gentiles to Christ, converting and baptizing everyone. For now, it means "participation," so that popes and bishops are *among*, not *above*, the people.

What has now become of the Second Vatican Council, almost sixty years after its closing? We would not be far off the mark if we ventured to respond, "everything and nothing." Those who make it to be everything always do so in view of a fundamental plan: finally to initiate and complete that process which, until yesterday, had been a mere pious intention.

Epilogue

Ten Long Years

Through the pages of this book, I have endeavored, for the sake of truth and for the love of theology, to trace the philosophical-theological roots of Pope Francis's teachings. What do we make of all this? We shall attempt to draw a conclusion by sketching a general consideration. These years of Pope Francis's pontificate have produced an anthropological revolution with undefined contours; liquid, as indeed liquid is also the apostasy plaguing the Church and harming the faith of the little ones. The radical change, or reformism, begins with a moral turn of no small magnitude, with *Amoris Lætitia* trying to widen the net of love.[239] Turning everything to love (a word rather than a reality) provoked a modification in finality that was baptized as a "paradigm shift": no longer the moral law as the sure way to the end, to the good, at the center of moral action, but love as the expression of mercy. When the truth of the moral law no longer preserves the truth of the human person from all abuses, it leads to moral indifferentism and the justification of a plurality of loves.

One of the most obvious effects of this Copernican revolution is the silent endorsement of the Lutheran thesis of sin at the

[239] I have discussed the moral implications of Pope Francis's teaching, especially the change of paradigm set forth by *Amoris Lætitia*, in my book *The Symphony of Truth: Theological Essays* (Waterloo, ON: Arouca Press, 2021).

core of being a man, which, in fact, results in the most boorish clericalism. Accepting sin as inevitable, resigning oneself to it, and then unhinging moral doctrine is the worst clericalism, since at this point the clergy have no supernatural purpose of healing man from deep within through the sacraments they minister. It seems that conversion is no longer required, but self-acceptance, accepting one's sin. One thus makes being dependent on sin. In truth, if sin is not redeemed, it is not redeemable either. Christ is simply a useless extra. He is that two-thousand-year-old Crucified One, dead with a death that Nietzsche wanted to see for Christian morality too.

Yet it is this very clericalism against which Nietzsche rightly rails, calling it the "morality of priests," i.e., a moralistic pretext for holding the souls of the simple, forcing them into submission to God and Christ because of a torturing awareness of sin. Nietzsche, however, as well as his new followers, ignore one fact: sin is redeemed, it is defeated; at the center of the salvific plan is Christ and the new man. Man's true greatness is his ability to be born again, recreated in Him through the gift of grace and charity.

A further step was next attempted. The "love *versus* law" dialectic led (with an almost ceaseless hammering, like the fact of being sinful) to making way for homosexual love and the LGBTQ+ culture, thus pushing the "love revolution" (or rather selfishness) to the edge of the precipice. By now it is clear that what is at stake is not how pastoral one can be, but the meaning attributed to what it is to be human.

Bishops fight against bishops over the immutable value of what God made by creating man. The U.S. bishops, on March 20, 2023, approved an excellent doctrinal note to draw the moral line at technologies that manipulate the human body with mutilation designed to change a person's sex ("gender"). They reiterate that what God did in creating man is a good thing and that it never yields a "being born in a wrong body." Body and soul are the whole man, and both express the image and likeness of God. Even the Scandinavian bishops, in a *Pastoral Letter on Human Sexuality* for Lent 2023, reiterate the non-negotiable truth of God the Creator's natural plan. The Church listens to everyone but does not negotiate its doctrine; the true face of God is at stake here, and therefore the true dignity of man is to be safeguarded against rainbow manipulations. Against these groups, the Belgian and German bishops took the field, deciding by majority vote to bless homosexual couples. Under the pretense of inclusion and pastoral care, they bless *de facto* the homosexualist ideology, dethroning divine Revelation. Homosexual acts now seem to have a right of citizenship, welcomed, like many other errors, under the merciful mantle of pastoral care.

Pope Francis' recent answer to one of the new dubia posed by five cardinals, in fact, hinted at the blessing of homosexual couples provided that any confusion with the sacrament of marriage is avoided—as if the Church could bless sin.[240]

This is truly something unheard of and unprecedented. Now the battle is being fought openly in the Church and not over an article of faith, such as, for example, at the time of Arianism, the theandric mystery of Christ, but over an even more basic issue, one which undergirds the Faith. Therefore, if this truth collapses, the edifice of Revelation inevitably collapses. At stake is the question of man as created by God and mankind's identity as male and female; marriage as a natural and supernatural covenant between man and woman, and therefore the Church as a spousal mystery.

[240] See www.vatican.va/roman_curia/congregations/cfaith/documents/rc_con_cfaith_risposta-dubia-2023_en.pdf.

If the complementarity between man and woman falls, *a fortiori* the typological-spousal signification of Christ and the Church falls. If the mystery-Church falls, the sacraments are abolished, grace is annulled, and much more besides, with a devastating domino effect, the preliminaries of which are already in *Amoris Lætitia.* This is an extremely serious situation. Behind the apparent mercy in blessing all kinds of love, because after all "love is love," is the anthropological lie of the man who wants to create himself, without God and against Him. It is resuscitated Eden, where the real teacher *ex cathedra* is the devil.

We are facing a revolution that lays hold of what is truly essential, natural, human. But like all revolutions that glory in the name, its cessation is never predictable. The one we face has gone even further. It does not stop at man. It next tries to replace human nature, created and redeemed man, with green nature, with trees and rivers. The anthropocentric turn of *Gaudium et Spes*, blessed by Paul VI, criticized during the Council by Karl Rahner but then promoted and developed explicitly by him in the post-conciliar period, is now just a rainbow reminiscence of cravings and instincts blessed with lots of holy water. At the center, however, is no longer man, certainly not Christ, but Mother Earth. Ecologism is the new soteriology, and climate change experts its prophets. Quite a few dioceses, for example, are now committed to becoming carbon neutral by 2030 in parishes and curial buildings. But whether people still go into these buildings seems not to be a matter of pastoral concern. Astonished, one wonders how it could have come to this. What went wrong at the philosophical-theological level to make possible proposing the salvation of the planet, the condemnation of "green sin," while opening the door to real sin and human misery? Christ is not there, but after all, His absence does not even seem that relevant to us. Christ has become a means to talk about something else. His name allows one to give oneself a name, Christian, in today's multicultural and syncretistic Areopagus, yet God seems to be *just* a name, one that comfortably brings together the most diverse religions. He Himself doesn't matter much anymore.

What has happened? Among the various things that have become entangled during this last half-century, we can find a starting point in the error of method above all (see the appendix below for further reflections on this point). The pastoral method, elevated to a principle in John XXIII's speech at the opening of Vatican II, has, over the long run, made doctrine into praxis. Conversely, praxis has become the only doctrine. The Church's teaching organ, the magisterium, was decanted into a learning organ when the "good pope," in that programmatic address, called for a magisterium with a more pastoral character.[241] Was the earlier magisterium not pastoral? Or had it not been sufficiently pastoral? What is the measure of true pastorality? No one knew, not even the pope.

Now we are faced with a slightly different problem, but it is a logical conclusion of that appeal: with the Synod on Synodality, the teaching body of the Church has become the student, while the student (the faithful), again by virtue of the same Synod, is

---

[241] See John XXIII, *Gaudet Mater Ecclesia*, *AAS* 54:785–95. In Latin (which was a translation from the original written in Italian), the pope's requests resounded thus: "Huic quippe modo plurimum tribuendum erit et patienter, si opus fuerit, in eo elaborandum; scilicet eæ inducendæ erunt rationes res exponendi, quæ cum magisterio, cuius indoles præsertim pastoralis est, magis congruent" (ibid, 792). The call was for a way (*modo*), a method, to be elaborated, in order to have a form of exposition more congruent with a magisterium whose nature is above all pastoral (*cuius indole præsertim pastoralis est*).

now the teaching body. It is a pyramidal revolution, Francis said, as we have seen, in which the base is at the top and the inverted top serves as the base. Some faithful say what they want, the bishops learn this and then vote with the faithful. Sheep of a lost flock who self-regulate by following the dictates of dominant thinking.

Ultimately, we seem to be trapped in a self-aggrandizing labyrinthine circle, where conciliar is synonymous with synodal, synodal synonymous with Church, and Church synonymous with the Second Vatican Council. Yes, the problem can be traced back to the beginning of Vatican II—to the desire to establish, with conciliar pastorality, a kind of "doctrine of method." The traditional notion of doctrine thus turned into a *way* of experience or experiment, a subjective method.

One might also ask what can be expected immediately after this revolution, which should now be called anthropo-naturalistic—anthropological with naturalistic implications. The aim is to overcome the fixity of human nature with the flexibility of simpler natural forms, such as those of vegetal life, which are portrayed as having a more intense contact with nature. What should we expect? Nothingness. But a liquid nothingness, one with indefinite, uncertain, non-describable boundaries about which there could be no science, but only stories. Narrative theology is in fact a new harbor of post-metaphysical theology or rather philosophy of religion. Perhaps we are already at this stage but we do not realize it. We have devolved into self-celebrating.

However, if there is still anyone who cares about Christ and His Church, the human person created by God, and what it means to be human—do something! Let your voice be heard. The alternative is to remain silent forever, swallowed up in the eddies of a nothingness that does not seem to be so, but is so.

Appendix

The Method Is the Problem

October 11, 2022, marked the sixtieth anniversary of the opening of the Second Vatican Council. After sixty years of the Council's aftermath, it seems very clear that beyond the various hermeneutic problems that have emerged, there is a fundamental juncture to examine carefully, an intersection where the conciliar paths meet even though they have opposing directions. I mean the problem of the method or way of expressing the Faith that was inaugurated by John XXIII's opening address. From Pope John XXIII to Pope Francis the distance is actually very short and not only because of a certain symmetry between the two. The unexpected reframing of a magisterium that is now presented as having a predominantly pastoral orientation was to be abundantly unfolded in the subsequent history and theology, until it found in Pope Francis an ideal sponsor and in some ways also a point of arrival. Everything that was only implicit before now becomes explicit.

John XXIII's introductory speech was so important that it was taken as having outlined a kind of "doctrine of method," and so Church teaching, as it had always been understood, easily became a *subjective* way and method. It is no secret that pastoral care as such has been elevated to the level of doctrine during these sixty postconciliar years. Thus, we continue to celebrate the Council as an "event" rather than as offering us teaching, as "spirit" rather than letter, that is, a body of texts. We are full of self-congratulation even while the Church burns down. The new method is precisely that. "Conciliar" is synonymous with "synodal"; "synodal" is synonymous with "Church"; and the Church is synonymous with the Second Vatican Council. There seems to be no escape from this self-congratulatory circle.

But let us proceed step by step and start from that orientating speech. Some might object that in doing so we are embracing a vision of rupture, dear to the disciples of Giuseppe Alberigo, and that we are reducing the Council to a speech, and furthermore, only the inaugural one; but let us proceed gradually so that the reader may follow our reasoning to its conclusion.

Let us start specifically from the programmatic speech, which is the true forerunner of the conciliar proceedings: *Gaudet Mater Ecclesia* of October 11, 1962. Among many other things, John XXIII said this, which became a kind of conciliar manifesto:

> What is needed is that this certain and unchangeable doctrine, to which loyal submission is due, be investigated and presented in the way demanded by our times. For the deposit of faith, the truths contained in our venerable doctrine, are one thing; the fashion in which they are expressed, but with the same meaning and the same judgement, is another thing. This way of speaking will require a great deal of work and, it may be, much patience: types of presentation must be introduced which are more in accord with a teaching authority that is primarily pastoral in character.[242]

---

[242] John XXIII, *Gaudet Mater Ecclesia*, no. 5, *AAS* 54:792.

Bear in mind that the text was entirely John XXIII's brainchild;[243] it was written in Italian[244] and then translated into Latin for the *Acta*.[245]

In a surprising and novel fashion, John XXIII goes on to distinguish between the deposit of faith or the truths contained in venerable doctrine, and the manner of enunciating them, while repeating that this (modern) manner was not to be an occasion to *change* doctrine by saying something else. In fact, St. Vincent of Lérins is quoted, who in his *Commonitorium* is the first to assert how a true development and amplification of doctrine is guaranteed in the continuity of principles and pronouncements, without true progress becoming a change (*mutatio*) and thus a corruption of doctrine. Here is the key passage from St. Vincent:

---

[243] See Peter Hebblethwaite, *John XXIII: Pope of the Council* (London: Geoffrey Chapman, 1984), 430; Andrea Riccardi, "The Tumultuous Opening Days of the Council," in Giuseppe Alberigo and Joseph A. Komonchak, eds., *History of Vatican II*, vol. 2: *The Formation of the Council's Identity. First Period and Intersession (October 1962–September 1963)* (Maryknoll: Orbis Books, 1997), 14–15.

[244] See Loris F. Capovilla, "Nel cuore della gente papa Giovanni è già santo," in *Jesus* 5 (1983): 64–72.

[245] Here is the Latin text of this passage, for the sake of accuracy: "Oportet ut hæc doctrina certa et immutabilis, cui fidele obsequium est præstandum, ea ratione pervestigetur et exponatur, quam tempora postulant nostra. Est enim aliud ipsum depositum Fidei, seu veritates, quæ veneranda doctrina nostra continentur, aliud modus, quo eadem enuntiantur, eodem tamen sensu eademque sententia. Huic quippe modo plurimum tribuendum erit et patienter, si opus fuerit, in eo elaborandum; scilicet eæ inducendæ erunt rationes res exponendi, quæ cum magisterio, cuius indoles præsertim pastoralis est, magis congruant." John XXIII, *Gaudet Mater Ecclesia*, no. 5, *AAS* 54:792.

If it is proper to progress that every reality should increase in itself, it is proper to change, on the other hand, that something should be transformed from one thing into another. It is therefore necessary that, with the passage of ages and centuries, there should grow and very vigorously progress the understanding, the knowledge, the wisdom as much of individuals as of all, as much of a single individual as of the whole Church—but only in its own kind, that is, in the same dogma, the same sense, and the same meaning [*sed in suo dumtaxat genere, in eodem scilicet dogmate, eodem sensu eademque sententia*].[246]

However, it seems that it was not so much *what* was said in the pope's speech but *how* it was said that was important. The *how* was to take precedence over the *what*. The emphasis was on the "how" of speaking, which had to be "pastoral." And yet, how could true progress of doctrine be guaranteed if the aim was not precisely doctrine, but the manner of expressing it? Isn't the manner of speaking, which cannot deviate an inch from the meaning and interpretation of the doctrine, simply incidental to the substance of the Faith? To say otherwise would be to introduce relativism.

In this way, the magisterium's center of gravity was going to be shifted, fixing it on the manner of expression, on the means. What was accidental would become essential and what is essential accidental. Taking a short leap forward to our own times, this would make it possible to be "inclusive" without having to bother about dogma, and to be open to novelty by favoring change but without attempting to justify it as such. Being "synodal" is now synonymous with inclusivity, listening to, and telling about

---

[246] St. Vincent of Lérins, *Commonitorium*, no. 23, in *CCL* 64:177–78.

the varied conditions of life, trying to effect a synthesis between what God made by creating man and what man makes of himself by excluding God. The desired change will not be a change in doctrine (at least not on center stage) but of the principle with which we *approach* it, which will then cause a subtle or insidious change in the doctrine. This will already be a change because *the way*, the approach, will be taken as a principle, and consequently the principle of faith will be taken as a way or an approach. The method of expressing the Faith, the way of believing, is implemented with a patience that aims at contriving the best way to stop saying uncomfortable or incomprehensible things to modern man, even though they had been so frequently reiterated in previous centuries. This "pastoral" approach has prevailed over the content of the Faith. The *fides qua* became dominant over the *fides quæ*—the subjective over the objective.

That opening speech, however, had a further aim. It aimed at adopting a form of teaching that would better suit the magisterium, one whose nature would be predominantly pastoral. As if to imply that the magisterium until then had not been pastoral enough! Now, the *subject*, that is, a person's natural inclination(s), had to be considered. In a new and clever way, the Pontiff was going to distinguish between doctrine and magisterium, placing the magisterium on the side of pastoral care—on the side of the way or method of proclaiming the Faith, and not on the side of the teaching of the doctrine of the Faith. Rightly understood, the "pastoral" is the field of experience under the guidance of faith and magisterium, the nature of which is primarily not pastoral, but didactic; if anything, we can say that the purpose of faith and magisterium is inherently pastoral, because it is aimed at the care of the faithful and their direction to Eternal Life. At least, that had been the case up to that point.

Yet, there occurred—in a prescient way, or as a lucid deduction from the premises?—a transformation of the teaching body into a learning body comprising experimentation, experience, and time. If the teacher becomes a schoolboy, the schoolboy will easily want to become a teacher. What happened a few years later with the rejection of authority was not a bolt out of the blue.[247]

It was certainly not Pope Roncalli who provoked the rebellion of '68. Yet those years were permeated with a spirit of self-redeeming optimism. Giuseppe Ruggieri notes: "A theologian would perhaps have something to say about this sharp distinction between presentation of doctrine and doctrine itself. But it was in any case the position of the *Gaudet Mater Ecclesia*."[248] What a magisterium with a pastoral character really meant no one managed to learn. Yet many began to gamble on that repositioning. The vagueness of the phrase was useful in creating a space for action for the Council Fathers, who remembered that "*Concilium Episcoporum est.*" *L'Osservatore Romano* highlighted that the primary purpose of John XXIII's speech was the defense and promotion of Catholic doctrine. *Le Monde*, on the other hand, was of the opinion that the pope had approved of the research methods used by modern thought. For *La Croix*, this speech was taken as a roadmap of Vatican II.[249] Was it a council of the media versus the Council of the Fathers, as Benedict XVI said in his last speech before retiring on February 14, 2013? Perhaps not. Instead, it seems it was the Fathers (at least one segment) and Roncalli

---

[247] Recall that the worldwide rejection of *Humanæ Vitæ* took place not quite six years after *Gaudet Mater Ecclesia* was pronounced.

[248] Giuseppe Ruggieri, "Il primo conflitto dottrinale," in Giuseppe Alberigo, ed., *Storia del concilio Vaticano II* (Bologna: Il Mulino, 1996), vol. 2: *La formazione della coscienza conciliare*, 281.

[249] See Riccardi, "Tumultuous Opening Days," 18.

himself who fueled the Council that was described by the popular media. Francis Sullivan observed that it was these words that set the tone for the whole Council agenda. Its exercise of teaching authority was to be overwhelmingly pastoral in character. What did that mean? While it was soothing that there were to be no more anathemas, nevertheless not everyone agreed on the notion of a "pastoral magisterium."[250]

It seems that with this discourse, Pope Roncalli was aiming above all at the pursuit of a new language to discover the presence of God in modern history. This was made manifest by the reason given for abandoning the classical way of formulating the doctrine of faith and morals in articles and with an anathema to ensure its clear reception. The Bride of Christ now preferred the medicine of mercy to the severity of condemning errors. Not because they were lacking—imagine!—but because men would repudiate them on their own when they turned toward the truth. This, indeed, is the atmosphere of optimism in which the Council took place. The new language, enunciated prophetically by the "good pope," would later be translated into in a multifaceted hermeneutical approach within the conciliar assembly regarding the very meaning of the pope's opening words—whether, for example, they

---

[250] "It was these last few words that set the tone and the agenda of the council. Its exercise of teaching authority was to be predominantly pastoral in character. But what did this mean? While most agreed that it meant there would be no anathemas, it soon appeared that there were very different notions of what was meant by a 'pastoral magisterium'" (Francis Sullivan, "Evaluation and Interpretation of the Documents of Vatican II," in *Creative Fidelity: Weighing and Interpreting Documents of the Magisterium* [Mahwah, NJ: Paulist Press, 1996], 163).

did not rule out altogether the "Roman theology" present in the preparatory schemas.

Later, the openness to a new and more pastoral language would favor a more narrative[251] and less systematic theology. Narrative allowed a distancing from a rigorous, deductive, scholastic or neoscholastic style. A more spontaneous, rhetorical, engaging thought, speech rich in metaphors, sometimes graced with poetic flourishes, comes to be preferred to argumentation. Iron logic gives way to "love," though not avoiding the risk of becoming loquacious and all-inclusive. Revealed truth will not be the starting point, a statement to be respected; rather it is to be, in a sense, a point of arrival. It is no longer a certainty but a possible achievement through the art of a fundamentally hermeneutical language. The symbolic link between Pope John XXIII's desiderata, with an openness to a less stilted style of speaking, and Pope Francis's description of Christian life as a "story to be told" is not hard to see. Francis, who loves metaphorical language and telling parables,[252] encourages the "narrative of life that becomes

---

[251] The expression "narrative theology" originated with the linguist Weinrich (Harald Weinrich, "Narrative Theology," in *Concilium* 5 [1973]: 139–56), supported by Metz's theological arguments (J.B. Metz, "Brief Apology for the Narrative," in *Concilium* 5 [1973]: 860–78). The latter invokes the narrated God, of Abraham, Isaac, and Jacob, rather than the God of philosophers and reason, appealing to a phrase of Pascal's. The endeavor of narrative theology is well summarized in a sentence by Karl Barth: "Wer und was Jesus Christus ist, das kann eben nur erzählt, nicht aber als ein System augeschaut und beschrieben werden" (Who is and what Jesus Christ is, can only be told and not grasped and defined as a system), quoted in Michael Schmaus, *Katholishe Dogmatik* (Munich: Max Hueber Verlag, 1955), vol. II/2, 206.

[252] See Gian Enrico Rusconi, *La teologia narrativa di papa Francesco* (Bari: Laterza, 2017), 4–30.

a story," since God has revealed Himself in His Incarnation and man is a storytelling being in the making, who discovers and is enriched in the stories of each day.[253] It was John XXIII with his new *modus operandi* that was to provide Francis with a policy for saying everything in a way that is always new and often contrary to his predecessors.

What is more, John XXIII's address served, in the opinion of many, as a structural vision of the new drafts that would replace the criticized preparatory schemas. In Congar's words, this inaugural address was a "discreet critique" of the supposedly negative view of the four dogmatic preparatory outlines (*De fontibus*, *De ordine morali*, *De deposito fidei*, and the *Formula nova professionis fidei*), whose sources were Trent, Vatican I, the encyclicals *Pascendi*, *Mediator Dei*, and *Humani Generis*, and the antimodernist decree *Lamentabili*.[254] It was the speech that the Bologna School[255] most frequently appealed to in order to make Vatican II "the council of John XXIII," one that Paul VI would later clip the wings of, when he shifted the emphasis to the ecclesiological datum. It

[253] See Pope Francis, Message for the 54th World Communications Day: "*That you may tell your children and grandchildren" (Ex 10:2): Life becomes history*, January 24, 2020, at www.vatican.va/content/francesco/en/messages/communications/documents/papa-francesco_20200124_messaggio-comunicazioni-sociali.html.

[254] See Yves Congar, "Erinnerungen an eine Episode auf dem II. Vatikanischen Konzil," in Elmar Klinger and Klaus Wittstadt, eds., *Glaube im Prozess: Christ nach dem II. Vatikanum* (Freiburg im Breisgau: Herder, 1984), 22.

[255] See Serafino M. Lanzetta, *Vatican II, A Pastoral Council: Hermeneutics of Council Teaching* (Leominster: Gracewing, 2016), xlvii–xlviii.

would be the way in which to continually revive Vatican II as an event rather than as a magisterial body of teaching.

Cardinal Bea, president of the Secretariat for Christian Unity, saw in the papal distinction between the content of the *depositum fidei* and the way of articulating it an important key to dialogue with Protestants; he saw it as fostering a welding together of pastoral form and ecumenical form in the documents to be composed.[256] An "event" had occurred—a new, disruptive event that would establish itself unquestioned as the Church's new Pentecost and would provide a way, at each anniversary, to relaunch Vatican II as the supreme council because of the fact that it *was* thus-and-such a kind of council and not because of what it taught or achieved. If the Faith and the Church are suffering a crisis of frightening dimensions, it seems that this does not matter much to the proponents of this point of view: the Council event now comes before the Faith. Roberto de Mattei writes:

> The Council had been convened, not to condemn errors or
> formulate new dogmas, but to propose, in language suited
> to the new times, the perennial teaching of the Church.
> The pastoral form, with John XXIII, became the form of
> the Magisterium par excellence. This perspective was des-
> tined, according to Alberigo, to make the Council an *event*,
> rather than a forum for the elaboration and production of
> norms. The main identity of Vatican II appeared to be that
> of "*aggiornamento*," understood as the "rejuvenation of the
> Christian life and of the Church" and the "readiness and

---

[256] Christoph Theobald, "Le opzioni teologiche del Vaticano II," in *Concilium* 4 (2005): 112–38, at 124.

attitude to seek a renewed inculturation of the Christian message in the new cultures."[257]

This perspective was bound to garner success as time went on, and especially today. In the name of the pastoral approach and the dialogue of Vatican II, other events have been promoted, personnel appointed, various readjustments made, all of which, heterodox in themselves, were nevertheless presented as examples of pastoral foresight. For example, the sponsorship of an idolatrous cult with Pachamama figurines during the Pan-Amazonian synod: in the name of what was this promoted, if not the freedom to engage a "natural wisdom" related to the earth and fertility, while crediting the value of a pagan cult? Then consider the recent and scandalous appointment to the Pontifical Academy for Life of economist Mariana Mazzucato, who has declared herself not only an atheist but strongly in favor of abortion. In the judgment of those who appointed her, what is at stake is not the thing itself—to be in favor of abortion or against it—but the manner in which one stands before the issue, which evidently neutralizes its importance as an issue. It is important only that "reflection" be elicited. If we were to ask Msgr. Vincenzo Paglia why he made this appointment, he would answer that abortion is not the point of it; Mazzucato is there for her economic talents. That's as clear as it gets! If John XXIII had reaffirmed with all his predecessors that magisterium is one thing and pastorality is another, interdependent but distinct, and if in the hall during Vatican II the new concept of pastoral magisterium had not begun to be canvassed from the very start, we would not—could not—have such aberrations and distortions as we do today. Not forgetting also those that happened in the

---

[257] Roberto de Mattei, *Il Concilio Vaticano II: Una storia mai scritta* (Turin: Lindau, 2010), 201–2.

pontificate of John Paul II, especially the various Assisi gather-ings in the name of peace, rather than in the Name of the true God Who gives us peace.

What is the result of all this? What is now seen as important is no longer what we must believe but *how* we are to believe—a privileging of consciousness over being, of the subject over God. Thus, even atheism is not stigmatized as unbelief but rather as a different, perhaps unselfconscious way of believing; and, therefore, a way of salvation can be found even for atheists. What matters is consciousness, not God; truth-telling or a sincere narrative, not the truth. Now *any* event can be treated like the council-event: natural and mundane or supernatural, as long as it bears some resemblance to the trademark "spirit of the Council."

"Ideas have consequences," declared the American scholar Richard Weaver.

Works Cited

Pope Francis

Address at the Commemorative Ceremony for the 50th Anniversary of the Institution of the Synod of Bishops, October 17, 2015; *AAS* 107 (2015): 1143.

Address to Conference on Pastoral Work for Vocations, on October 21, 2016. *AAS* 11 (2016).

Address to the Ecumenical Delegation of the Patriarchate of Constantinople, June 27, 2015.

Address to the Faithful of the Diocese of Rome, September 18, 2021. *L'Osservatore Romano*, September 18, 2021.

Address to the Italian Theological Association, December 29, 2017. *AAS* 110 (2018).

Address to Participants in the Meeting Promoted by the National Catechetical Office of the Italian Episcopal Conference, January 30, 2021. *L'Osservatore Romano*, January 30, 2021.

Address to Participants in the Meeting Promoted by the Pontifical Council for Promoting the New Evangelization, October 11, 2017. *L'Osservatore Romano*, October 13, 2017.

Address to Participants in the 68th National Liturgical Week, August 24, 2017. *L'Osservatore Romano*, August 25, 2017.

Address to Meeting on the Protection of Minors in the Church, February 24, 2019. *L'Osservatore Romano*, February 25–26, 2019.

Amoris Laetitia. Post-synodal Apostolic Exhortation. March 19, 2016.

Angelus of February 14, 2021. *L'Osservatore Romano*, February 15, 2021.

Conversation with the Jesuits of Chile, on January 16, 2018. www. vatican.va/content/francesco/it/speeches/2018/january/documents/ papa-francesco_20180116_cile-santiagogesuiti.html.

Document on Human Fraternity for World Peace and Living Together (with Sheikh Ahmed el-Tayeb, Grand Imam of Al-Azhar), Abu Dhabi, February 4, 2019. *L'Osservatore Romano*, February 4–5, 2019.

Episcopalis Communio. Motu proprio of September 15, 2018.

Evangelii Gaudium. Apostolic Exhortation on the Proclamation of the Gospel. November 24, 2013. *AAS* 105 (2013).

Fratelli Tutti. Encyclical Letter. October 4, 2020. *AAS* 112.

General Audience on Wednesday, March 27, 2013. *L'Osservatore Romano*, March 28, 2013.

Homily "Judas, where are you?," April 8, 2020.

"'I believe the Lord wants a change in the Church': A private dialogue with the Jesuits in the Baltics." *La Civiltà Cattolica* (2018), IV, 105– 13; www.laciviltacattolica.com/i-believe-the-lord-wants-a-change-in-the-church-a-private-dialogue-with-the-jesuits-in-the-baltics/.

Interview with Fr. Antonio Spadaro, September 19, 2013. *Civiltà Cattolica* (2013) III, 449–77; www.laciviltacattolica.it/articolo/intervista-a-papa-francesco/. English translation: www.americamagazine.org/ faith/2013/09/30/big-heart-open-god-interview-pope-francis.

Laudato Si'. Encyclical Letter on Care for Our Common Home. June 18, 2015. *AAS* 107.

Letter to the Bishops of the Whole World that Accompanies the Apostolic Letter Motu Proprio *Traditionis Custodes* on the Use of the Roman Liturgy Prior to the Reform of 1970, July 16, 2021. *L'Osservatore Romano* on July 16, 2021

Message for the 54th World Communications Day: *"That you may tell your children and grandchildren" (Ex 10:2): Life becomes history*, January 24, 2020.

Misericordiæ Vultus. Apostolic Letter. April 11, 2015.

Moment of Reflection for the Beginning of the Synodal Journey. *L'Osservatore Romano*, October 9, 2021.

Works Cited

Morning Meditation in the Domus Sanctæ Marthæ Chapel, September 9, 2016. *L'Osservatore Romano*, September 10, 2016.

Our Father: Reflections on the Lord's Prayer. New York: Image, 2018.

Press conference on the return flight from Abu Dhabi, February 5, 2019, at: www.vatican.va/content/francesco/it/speeches/2019/february/documents/papa-francesco_20190205_emiratiarabi-voloritorno.html.

Rescript: New revision to number 2267 of the Catechism of the Catholic Church on the death penalty. *L'Osservatore Romano*, August 1, 2018. For the Pontifical Rescript and the Letter to the Bishops of the CDF, see: https://press.vatican.va/content/salastampa/it/bollettino/pubblico/2018/08/02/0556.pdf.

Traditionis Custodes. Apostolic Letter on the Use of the Roman Liturgy Prior to the Reform of 1970, July 16, 2021. *L'Osservatore Romano*, July 16, 2021

Urbi et Orbi Prayer Service. *L'Osservatore Romano*, March 29, 2020.

Welcome to Participants in the General Assembly of the Focolare Movement, September 26, 2014. *L'Osservatore Romano*, September 27, 2014.

Without Jesus We Can Do Nothing: Being a Missionary in the World Today. A Conversation with Gianni Valente. New London, CT: Twenty-Third Publications, 2020.

OTHER CHURCH DOCUMENTS & WRITINGS BY POPES

Benedict XVI, "The Church and the Scandal of Sexual Abuse." April 10, 2019. www.catholicnewsagency.com/news/41013/full-text-of-benedict-xvi-essay-the-church-and-the-scandal-of-sexual-abuse.

———. *Declaratio Summi Pontificis—De muneris Episcopi Romæ, Successoris Sancti Petri abdicatione*, in *AAS* 105 (2013): 239.

———, and Robert Cardinal Sarah. *From the Depths of Our Hearts: Priesthood, Celibacy and the Crisis of the Catholic Church.* San Francisco: Ignatius Press, 2020.

———. General Audience, October 18, 2006.

———. General Audience, February 27, 2013. *Insegnamenti di Benedetto XVI*, vol. 9 (Vatican City: Libreria Editrice Vaticana, 2013), 271–72.

———. *Jesus of Nazareth: From the Baptism in the Jordan to the Transfiguration*. London: Bloomsbury, 2007.

———. *The Origins of the Church: The Apostles and Their Co-Workers*. San Francisco: Ignatius Press, 2010.

Catchism of the Catholic Church.

Codex Iuris Canonici (1917).

Codex Iuris Canonici (1983).

Congregation for the Doctrine of Faith. Instruction *Donum Veritatis*. May 24, 1990. *AAS* 82 (1990).

———. *The Primacy of the Successor of Peter in the Mystery of the Church*. *L'Osservatore Romano*, October 31, 1998.

———. *Professio fidei et Iusiurandum fidelitatis*. *AAS* 81 (1989).

Innocent III. Sermo II: In consecratione Pontificis Maximi. PL 217.

John XXIII. *Gaudet Mater Ecclesia*. Address for the Solemn Opening of the Second Vatican Council. October 11, 1962.

John Paul II. *Crossing the Threshold of Hope*. London: Jonathan Cape, 1994.

———. *Dives in Misericordia*. Encyclical Letter. November 30, 1980.

———. *Ecclesia de Eucharistia*. Encyclical Letter. April 17, 2003.

———. *Redemptoris Missio*. Encyclical Letter. December 7, 1990.

———. *Ut Unum Sint*. Encyclical Letter on Commitment to Ecumenism. May 25, 1995. *AAS* 87 (1995).

Pius IX. *Mirabilis Illa Constantia*. Letter to the Bishops of Germany, March 4, 1875.

Vatican Council I. *Pastor Æternus*. Dogmatic Constitution on the Church of Christ. July 18, 1870.

Vatican Council II. *Ad Gentes*. Decree on Missionary Activity. December 7, 1965.

———. *Christus Dominus*. Decree on the Pastoral Office of Bishops. October 28, 1965.

Works Cited

———. *Gaudium et Spes.* Pastoral Constitution on the Church in the Modern World. December 7, 1965.

———. *Lumen Gentium.* Dogmatic Constitution on the Church. November 21, 1964.

———. *Sacrosanctum Concilium.* Constitution on the Sacred Liturgy. December 4, 1963.

———. *Unitatis Redintegratio.* Decree on Ecumenism. November 21, 1964.

Fathers and Doctors of the Church

Ambrose, *Exameron.* PL 14.

———. *Hymni.* PL 17.

Anselm. *Proslogion.* Translation in Brian Davies and G.R. Evans, ed., *Anselm of Canterbury: The Major Works.* Oxford: Oxford University Press, 2008.

Augustine. *De civitate Dei.* Translation cited: *The City of God Books XVII–XXII*, trans. Gerald G. Walsh, SJ, and Daniel J. Honan. *The Fathers of the Church*, vol. 24. Washington, DC: Catholic University of America Press, 1954.

———. *Retractationes, Contra epistulam Donati heretici liber unus.* Translated by M. Inez Bogan. *The Fathers of the Church*, vol. 60. Washington, DC: The Catholic University of America Press, 1968.

———. *Sermo 76.* Translated (as *Sermon 26*) by Philip Schaff, ed. *Nicene and Post-Nicene Fathers*, vol. 6. Peabody, MA: Hendrickson, 1995.

Bonaventure. *In IV Sententiarum.*

Catherine of Siena. *The Dialogue of the Seraphic Virgin Catherine of Siena.*

Cyprian. *De catholicæ Ecclesiæ unitatæ.* PL 4.

John Chrysostom. *Homily on the Letter to the Hebrews.* PG 63.

Leo the Great. *Sermo 3: De Natali ipsius; habitus in anniversario die assumptionis eiusdem ad summi pontificii munus.* In *The Fathers of the Church*, vol. 93. Translated Jane Patricia Freeland and Agnes Josephine Conway. Washington, DC: The Catholic University of America Press, 1996.

————. *Sermo 62, De Passione Domini XI.*

Origen, *Commentaria in Evangelium secundum Matthæum.* PG 13.

————. *De principiis.* PG 11.

Tertullian, *De præscriptione hæreticorum.* PL 2.

Thomas Aquinas, *Catena Aurea: Commentary on the Four Gospels.* Vol. III, St. Luke. London: Baronius Press, 2017.

————. *In IV Sententiarum.*

————. *Quaestiones disputatae De veritate.*

————. *Super Matthaeum.*

————. *Summa theologiæ.*

Vincent of Lérins, *Commonitorium.* PL 50.

Additional Sources

Anonymous. *Decretum.* PL 107.

Aslan, Ednan, and Marcia Hermansen, eds. *Religion and Violence: Muslim and Christian Theological and Pedagogical Reflections.* Wiesbaden: Springer, 2017.

Boni, Geraldina. *La recente attività normativa ecclesiale: 'finis terræ' per lo 'ius canonicum'? Per una valorizzazione del ruolo del Pontificio Consiglio per i testi legislativi e della scienza giuridica nella Chiesa.* Modena: Mucchi, 2021.

Borghesi, Massimo. *Jorge Mario Bergoglio: Una biografia intellettuale.* Milan: Jaca Book, 2017. English edition: *The Mind of Pope Francis: Jorge Mario Bergoglio's Intellectual Journey.* Translated by Barry Hudock. Collegeville: Liturgical Press, 2018.

Braun, Herbert. *An die Hebräer.* Tübingen: Mohr, 1984.

Bruce, F.F. *The Epistle to the Hebrews.* Grand Rapids, MI: Eerdmans, 1964.

Bruno of Segni. *Commentary on Matthew.* PL 165.

Calmel, Roger-Thomas. *Breve Apologia della Chiesa di sempre.* Albano Laziale: Ichthys, 2007.

Capovilla, Loris F. "Nel cuore della gente papa Giovanni è già santo." *Jesus* 5 (1983): 64–72.

Works Cited

Casalini, Nello. *Agli Ebrei: Discorso di esortazione.* Jerusalem: Franciscan Printing Press, 1992.

Chenaux, Philippe. "Il primato petrino nel contesto del Vaticano I." *Lateranum* 87, no. 1 (2021).

Coda, Piero. *La Chiesa è il vangelo—Alle sorgenti della teologia di papa Francesco.* Vatican City: Libreria Editrice Vaticana, 2017.

Congar, Yves. "Erinnerungen an eine Episode auf dem II. Vatikanischen Konzil." In *Glaube im Prozess: Christ nach dem II. Vatikanum*, ed. Elmar Klinger and Klaus Wittstadt. Freiburg im Breisgau: Herder, 1984.

———. "Konzils als Versammlung und grundsätzliche Konziliarität der Kirche." In *Gott in Welt: Festgabe für Karl Rahner*, J.B. Metz, W. Kern, A. Darlapp, H. Vorgrimler, eds., vol. II, 135–65. Freiburg: Herder, 1964.

———. "Note sul Concilio come assemble e sulla conciliarità fondamentale della Chiesa." In *Orizzonti attuali della teologia*, vol. II. Rome: Edizioni Paoline, 1967.

———. *Vera e falsa riforma nella Chiesa.* Milan: Jaca Book, 1994.

Cullmann, Oscar. *Peter, Disciple-Apostle-Martyr: A Historical and Theological Study.* London: SCM Press, 1953.

Czerny, Card. Michael, and Christian Barone. *Siblings All, Sign of the Times: The Social Teaching of Pope Francis.* With a preface by Pope Francis. Maryknoll, NY: Orbis Books, 2022.

Dalla Torre, Giuseppe. *Papi di famiglia. Un secolo di servizio alla Santa Sede.* Venice: Marcianum Press, 2020.

de Lubac, Henri. *The Splendour of the Church.* London: Sheed and Ward, 1956.

de Mattei, Roberto. *Il Concilio Vaticano II: Una storia mai scritta.* Turin: Lindau, 2010. English edition: *The Second Vatican Council: An Unwritten Story.* Translated by Patrick T. Brannan, Michael J. Miller, and Kenneth D. Whitehead. Fitzwilliam, NH: Loreto Publications, 2012.

———, ed. *Il modernismo: radici e conseguenze storiche*, in *Vecchio e nuovo modernismo: Radici della crisi nella Chiesa.* Rome: Fiducia, 2020.

———. *Love for the Papacy and Filial Resistance to the Pope in the History of the Church*. Brooklyn, NY: Angelico Press, 2019.

———. *Vicario di Cristo: Il primato tra normalità ed eccezione*. 2nd ed. Verona: Fede & Cultura, 2018.

De Ruggiero, Guido. *La filosofia contemporanea*, vol. II. Bari: Laterza, 1947.

De Wulf, Maurice. "Nominalism." *The Catholic Encyclopedia*, vol. 11. New York: Robert Ampleton Company, 1911.

Dianich, Severino S. *Per una teologia del Papato*. San Paolo: Cinisello Balsamo, 2010.

Di Corrado, Giuseppe. *Pietro pastore della Chiesa negli scritti di Agostino d'Ippona*. Roma: Città Nuova, 2012.

Dounot, Cyrille. "Une solution de continuité doctrinale. Peine de mort et enseignement de l'Église." *Catholica* 141 (2018): 46–73.

Dublanchy, E. "Infallibilité du pape." *Dictionnarie de théologie catholique*, vol. 7. Paris: Letouzey et Ané, 1927.

Francis of Assisi. *Fonti Francescane: Scritti e biografie di san Francesco d'Assisi, Cronache e altre testimonianze del primo secolo francescano; Scritti e biografie di santa Chiara d'Assisi*. Edited by Ernesto Caroli. Padua: Edizioni Messaggero Padova, 1996.

Gherardini, Brunero. *La Chiesa: mistero e servizio* (Rome: EDUSC, 1994)

Gaillardetz, Richard. "The 'Francis Moment': A New Kairos for Catholic Ecclesiology." *Proceedings of the Catholic Theological Society of America* 69 (2014): 75–80.

Gianfranco Ghirlanda, "Cessazione dall'ufficio di Romano Pontefice," in *La Civiltà Cattolica*, March 2, 2013, pp. 445–62.

Giuliani, Veronica (Saint). *Un tesoro nascosto. Diario*, vol. III. Città di Castello: Monastero delle Cappuccine, 1973.

Glenn, Paul J. *The History of Philosophy*. London: B. Herder Book Co., 1948.

Gottwald, Norman K. "The Exodus as Event and Process: A Test Case in the Biblical Grounding of Liberation Theology. In *The Future of Liberation Theology: Essays in Honor of Gustavo Gutiérrez*, ed. M.H. Ellis and O. Maduro, 250–60. Maryknoll, NY: Orbis Books, 1989.

Works Cited

Grillo, Andrea. "Superare lo stato di eccezione liturgica: restituire autorita alla *lex orandi* e ai vescovi. In *Oltre "Summorum Pontificum": Per una riconciliazione liturgica possibile*, ed. A. Grillo and Z. Carra, 67–76. Bologna: EDB, 2020.

Gutiérrez, Gustavo. *A Theology of Liberation: History, Politics, and Salvation.* Maryknoll, NY: Orbis Books, 1988.

Hebblethwaite, Peter. *John XXIII: Pope of the Council.* London: Geoffrey Chapman, 1984.

Hume, David. *Dialogues on Natural Religion.* Edited by Jonathan Bennett (2017) at www.earlymoderntexts.com/.

Insero, Walter. *Il popolo secondo Francesco: Una rilettura ecclesiologica.* Vatican City: Libreria Editrice Vaticana, 2018.

Ivo of Chartres. *Decretales.* PL 161:330.

Journet, Charles. *L'Église du Verbe incarné.* Volume 1: *La hiérarchie apostolique.* Saint-Maurice: Édition Saint-Augustin, 1998.

Kasper, Walter. *Misericordia: Concetto fondamentale del vangelo—Chiave della vita.* Brescia: Queriniana, 2013.

———. *Papa Francesco: La rivoluzione della tenerezza e dell'amore.* Brescia: Queriniana, 2015.

Kwasniewski, Peter. "Andrea Grillo: The Mind Behind the Motu Proprio." *OnePeterFive*, August 18, 2021.

———. "Damned Lies: On the Destiny of Judas Iscariot." *Rorate Caeli*, March 30, 2015.

———. "Objections and Replies on 'Pastor Æternus.'" *OnePeterFive*, May 10, 2023.

Lafont, Ghislain. *Piccolo saggio sul tempo di Papa Francesco.* Bologna: Edizioni Dehoniane, 2017.

Lamont, John R.T., and Claudio Pierantoni. *Defending the Faith against Present Heresies.* Waterloo, ON: Arouca Press, n.d.

Lanzetta, Serafino M. "Il carattere 'pastorale' del Vaticano II tra interpretazioni coerenti (cioè logiche) e interpretazioni incoerenti (cioè arbitrarie)." *Divinitas Verbi: Quaderni di epistemologia teologica (Teologia e Magistero oggi)* 1 (2017): 27–58.

———. "La misericordia secondo il Card. W. Kasper." *Fides Catholica* 1 (2016): 185–89.

———. *The Symphony of Truth: Theological Essays.* Waterloo, ON: Arouca Press, 2021.

———. *Il Vaticano II un concilio pastorale. Ermeneutica delle dottrine conciliari.* Siena: Cantagalli, 2014.

———. *Vatican II, A Pastoral Council: Hermeneutics of Council Teaching.* Leominster: Gracewing, 2016.

Lebra, Andrea. "Papa Francesco e il Vaticano II." *SettimanaNews*, February 26, 2018, www.settimana news.it/chiesa/papa-francesco-vaticano-ii.

Livi, Antonio. "Il pancristismo materialistico di Teilhard de Chardin," https://cooperatoresveritatis.files.wordpress.com/2015/04/il-pan-cristismo-materialistico-di-teilhard-de-chardin.pdf.

Löser, Werner. *Im Geiste des Origenes: Hans Urs von Balthasar als Interpret der Theologie der Kirchenväter.* Frankfurt: Knecht, 1976.

Mallon, James. *Divine Renovation: Bringing Your Parish from Maintenance to Mission.* New London, CT: Twenty-Third Publications, 2014.

Metz, J.B. "Brief Apology for the Narrative." *Concilium* 5 (1973): 860–78.

Moriconi, Bruno. *Farsi prossimo: Meditazioni sulla parabola del Buon Samaritano.* Rome: Città Nuova, 2006.

Mucci, Giandomenico. "L'inferno vuoto." *La Civiltà Cattolica* (2008) II, 132–38.

Müller, Gerhard. *Der Papst: Sendung und Auftrag.* Freiburg: Verlag Herder, 2017.

———. "Kardinal Müller zu Machen der Kurienreform: 'Theologische Ahnungslosigkeit.'" Interview with *Passauer Neue Presse*, May 6, 2019.

Navarre Bible. *The Letter to the Hebrews.* Dublin: Four Courts Press, 2003.

Newman, John Henry. *An Essay on the Development of Christian Doctrine.* London: James Toovey, 1845.

Nietzsche, Friedrich. *Human, All-Too-Human.* Translated by Helen Zimmern. London: T.N. Foulis, 1910.

O'Malley, John W. *Vatican I: The Council and the Making of the Ultra-montane Church.* Cambridge, MA: The Belknap Press, 2018.

Works Cited

Ott, Ludwig. *Fundamentals of Catholic Dogma.* Cork: The Mercier Press, 1958.

Pentin, Edward. "Key Synod Father: Pan-Amazon Synod 'May Be a Step to' Women Catholic Priests." *National Catholic Register*, October 9, 2019.

Perroni, Marinella. *Kerigma e profezia: L'ermeneutica biblica di papa Francesco.* Vatican City: Libreria Editrice Vaticana, 2017.

Pighi, Alberto. *Hierarchiæ ecclesiasticæ assertio.* Cologne, 1538.

Rahner, Karl. *Foundations of Christian Faith: An Introduction to the Idea of Christianity.* Translated by William V. Dych. New York: Crossroad, 2016.

Ratzinger, Joseph. "L'ecclesiologia della Costituzione *Lumen gentium.*" In *Il Concilio Vaticano II: Recezione e attualità alla luce del Giubileo*, ed. Rino Fisichella, 66–82. San Paolo: CiniSello Balsamo, 2000.

———. *Popolo e Casa di Dio in S. Agostino.* Milan: Jaca Book, 1978.

Ravasi, Gianfranco. "Sul 'monitum' del 1962 riguardante Teilhard de Chardin," www.cultura.va/content/dam/cultura/docs/comunicati-stampa/CS23nov10Teilhard.pdf.

Repole, Roberto. *Il sogno di una Chiesa evangelica—L'ecclesiologia di Papa Francesco* (Vatican City: Libreria Editrice Vaticana, 2017), 31.

Riccardi, Andrea. *La Chiesa brucia. Crisi e futuro del cristianesimo.* Bari: Laterza, 2021.

———. *Il cristianesimo al tempo di papa Francesco.* Bari: Laterza, 2018.

———. "The Tumultuous Opening Days of the Council." In *History of Vatican II*, vol. 2: *The Formation of the Council's Identity. First Period and Intersession (October 1962–September 1963)*, ed. Giuseppe Alberigo and Joseph A. Komonchak. Maryknoll: Orbis Books, 1997.

Ruggieri, Giuseppe. "Il primo conflitto dottrinale." In *Storia del concilio Vaticano II*, vol. 2: *La formazione della coscienza conciliare*, ed. Giuseppe Alberigo. Bologna: Il Mulino, 1996.

Rusconi, Gian Enrico. *La teologia narrativa di papa Francesco.* Bari: Laterza, 2017.

Salaverri, Joachim. *De Ecclesia Christi.* In *Sacra Theologiæ Summa*, vol. 1. Madrid: B.A.C., 1958.

Sarto, Blanco. "Mysterium, communio et Sacramentum. La Ecclesiologia eucaristica di Joseph Ratzinger." *Annales Theologici* 25 (2011): 241–70.

Scannone, Juan Carlos. "La filosofia dell'azione di Blondel e l'agire di Papa Francesco." *La Civiltà Cattolica* (2015) IV, 216–33.

Schmaus, Michael. *Katholishe Dogmatik.* Munich: Max Hueber Verlag, 1955.

Schneider, Athanasius. "On the Question of a Heretical Pope." *OnePeter-Five*, March 20, 2019.

———. "On the question of the true pope in the light of the opinion of the automatic loss of the papal office for heresy and the speculations about the resignation of Benedict XVI." *OnePeterFive*, February 28, 2020.

———. "On the Validity of Pope Francis." *OnePeterFive*, September 19, 2023.

Sheen, Fulton. *The Priest Is Not His Own.* London: Peter Davies, 1963.

Siano, Paolo M. *Un manuale per conoscere la massoneria.* Frigento: Casa Mariana Editrice, 2012.

———. *La massoneria tra esoterismo, ritualità e simbolismo.* Volume 1. Frigento: Casa Mariana Editrice, 2012.

Silveira, Arnaldo Xavier da. *Two Timely Issues: The New Mass and the Possibility of a Heretical Pope.* Translated by John Russell Spann and José Aloisio Schelini. Spring Grove, PA: The Foundation for a Christian Civilization, 2022.

Stenico, Tommaso. *Il Concilio Vaticano II: Carisma e profezia* (Milan: Finoia, 2020)

Sullivan, Francis. *Creative Fidelity: Weighing and Interpreting Documents of the Magisterium.* Mahwah, NJ: Paulist Press, 1996.

Teilhard de Chardin, Pierre. *The Future of Man.* London: William Collins Sons & Co., 1964.

———. *Writings in Time of War.* London: Collins, 1968.

Works Cited

Theobald, Christoph. "L'exhortation apostolique *Evangelii gaudium*. Esquisse d'une interprétation originale du Concile Vatican II." *Revue Théologique de Louvain* 46 (2015): 321–40.

———. *Fraternità—Il nuovo stile della Chiesa secondo papa Francesco*. Magnano: Edizioni Qiqajon, 2016.

———. "Le opzioni teologiche del Vaticano II." *Concilium* 4 (2005): 112–38.

———. "The Theological Options of Vatican II: Seeking an 'Internal' Principle of Interpretation." *Concilium* 4 [English] (2005): 87–107.

Tomberg, Valentin. *Meditation on the Tarot: A Journey into Christian Hermeticism*. New York: TarcherPerigree, 1985.

Torquemada, Juan de. *Summa de Ecclesia*. Rome, 1469.

Trapè, Agostino. "La 'Sedes Petri' in S. Agostino." In *Miscellanea Antonio Piolanti*, vol. II, 1–19. Rome: Facultas Theologiæ Pontificiæ Universitatis Lateranensis, 1964.

Violi, Stefano. "La rinuncia di Benedetto XVI tra storia, diritto e coscienza." *Rivista Teologica di Lugano* 18, no. 2 (2013): 203–14.

von Balthasar, Hans Urs. *Dare We Hope "That All Men Be Saved"?* San Francisco: Ignatius Press, 2014.

———. *The Theology of Henri de Lubac*. San Francisco: Ignatius Press, 1991.

———. "Who is the Church?" In *Explorations in Theology*, vol. II: *Spouse of the Word*. San Francisco: Ignatius Press, 1991.

Weigel, George. *The Next Pope. The Office of Peter and a Church in Mission*. San Francisco: Ignatius Press, 2020.

Weinrich, Harald. "Narrative Theology." *Concilium* 5 (1973): 139–56.

Zani, Angelo Vincenzo. "La responsabilità della teologia per una Chiesa 'in uscita.'" *Teologia* 42 (2017): 3–22.

Index of Names

Index of Names

About the Author

Fr Serafino Maria Lanzetta is a Marian Franciscan based in the diocese of Portsmouth in the United Kingdom. He holds a doctorate in Sacred Theology and a post-doctoral habilitation in ecclesiology. He is lecturer in Systematic Theology at St Mary's University Twickenham, London, and at the Theological Faculty of Lugano (Switzerland). He is an author of many articles and books, and a broadcaster.

You might enjoy some other titles published by Os Justi Press:

Dogmatic Theology
Lattey (ed.), *The Incarnation*
Lattey (ed.), *St Thomas Aquinas*
Pohle, *God: His Knowability, Essence, and Attributes*
Pohle, *The Author of Nature and the Supernatural*
Scheeben, *A Manual of Catholic Theology* (2 vols.)
Scheeben, *Nature and Grace*

Spiritual Theology
Doyle, *Vocations*
Guardini, *Sacred Signs*
Leen, *The True Vine and Its Branches*
Swizdor, *God in Me*

Liturgy
A Benedictine Martyrology
The Life of Worship
The Roman Martyrology (Pocket Edition)
Chaignon, *The Sacrifice of the Mass Worthily Offered*
Croegaert, *The Mass: A Liturgical Commentary* (2 vols.)
Kwasniewski (ed.), *John Henry Newman on Worship, Reverence, and Ritual*
Parsch, *The Breviary Explained*
Pothier, *Cantus Mariales*
Shaw, *Sacred and Great*

Language & Literature
The Little Flowers of Saint Francis (illustrated)
Brittain, *Latin in Church*
Farrow, *Pageant of the Popes*
Kilmer, *Anthology of Catholic Poets*
Lazu Kmita, *The Island Without Seasons*
Papini, *Gog*
Walsh, *The Catholic Anthology*

Printed in Great Britain
by Amazon